Tom Butler's Schooldays

The Memoirs of a Christ's Hospital pupil, 1853-61

Edited by Charlie Butler

INTRODUCTION

First Edition: 2011
Copyright Charlie Butler and Naomi Alexander
ISBN: 978-1-4476-6802-2
Published by Lulu.com

INTRODUCTION

Thomas Robinson Butler in his Christ's Hospital uniform, c.1854

Thomas Robinson Butler was born at 6, Cheyne Walk, Chelsea, on 10th June 1846, into a family with a strong educational and religious tradition.

The Butler family had lived at the address since the 1770s, when Thomas Robinson's great-grandfather, Rev. Weeden Butler (1742-1823), began to run a classical school from the house. The school was successful, and passed in due course to Weeden's son (1772-1831), who was also a clergyman and also called Weeden. The younger Weeden maintained it into the 1820s, numbering among his pupils the young Isambard Kingdom Brunel. On his death the house was inherited by his son Thomas Butler (1809-1907). Unlike the two Weedens, Thomas did not enter the church or education but spent his long career at the British Museum, of which he became in due course Assistant Secretary. He married Jane Isabella North in 1837, and with her raised ten children to adulthood, of whom Thomas Robinson, whose memoir this is, was the sixth.

INTRODUCTION

In her memoir of their father, *Nearly a Hundred Years Ago*, Thomas Robinson's elder sister Annie Robina described life in Cheyne Walk during Thomas Robinson's early childhood:

> Cheyne Walk faced the river Thames. At exceptionally high tides it was flooded, to the extreme delight of the younger members of the household at No.6, who ran on improvised bridges and sailed their paper boats down the long passages, and fancied themselves in Venice. The elders appreciated the experience less, and typhoid was no stranger at No.6 before the days of the Embankment.
>
> The walls of the house were oak panelled, in some cases up to lofty ceilings; the deep window seats behind heavy curtains seemed made expressly for little ones, catlike, to curl themselves up in. There they could read or learn lessons undisturbed, and in those window seats, or "lockers", they could keep anything they liked. An old oak staircase, with low wide stairs, faced the front hall.
>
> There were between twenty and thirty rooms in this house, many of them in suites and of palatial size. It would have been impossible to think of filling them oneself, however rapidly one's family might grow. But suites with their own kitchens could be let, and one of them was already a haunt of the scientific world. The names of Baden-Powell, Bonomi and Flinders always sound strangely familiar to us, as echoes from our infancy. Another suite was given up to the clergyman of our parish, the Rev. William W. Robinson, at that time the only teetotal clergyman in London, and "the greatest Tractarian in England" as he delighted to tell us; *i.e.* he gave away the largest number of tracts—which tracts we children used to fold up for him in fanciful shapes. (*Nearly a Hundred Years Ago* (1907), 86-87.)

As this picture suggests, the milieu in which Thomas Robinson grew up was at once academic, clerical and scientific. His father's cousins included a future Master of Trinity, Cambridge, and (by marriage) both the social reformer Josephine Butler and the scientist Francis Galton. The atmosphere of Thomas

INTRODUCTION

Butler's own house, both at Cheyne Walk and later in Holborn (where the family moved in the 1850s) was a peculiarly-Victorian mixture of scientific curiosity and religious piety. Of Thomas Robinson's own siblings two, like him, went on to be ordained; one was an expert in Magyar philology; one a naturalist with a specialism in birds and butterflies who was consulted for his expertise by Darwin. Both Thomas Robinson's immediate younger siblings, Frank and Fanny, became doctors. Frank went on to enjoy a successful second career as a mineralogist, while Fanny, one of the first Englishwomen to qualify as a doctor, became a medical missionary and died in Kashmir in 1889.

Thomas Robinson did not share the intellectual brilliance of some of his relations. The man who emerges from these pages is scrupulously honest and blessed with a prodigious memory, but seems also a little unworldly. For a memoirist, however, this is a valuable combination of qualities, and the result may be more reliable than an account produced by a more artful writer. After leaving Christ's Hospital Thomas Robinson attended Highgate College, which had recently become a Church of England seminary. He was ordained deacon in 1869, and priest the following year. After that his professional life consisted of a long series of curacies, in Macclesfield, Manchester, Bethnal Green, Stratford (London), Fareham, Wiltshire, Kent, Frome and Bristol amongst other places. It was in 1881, while he was curate of St John's Church, Stratford, that he married Maria Stockdale, with whom he went on to have two sons, Montagu Christie (known to the family as Christie) (1884-1970) and Guido Wilfred (1886-1956). Perhaps with his experience at Christ's Hospital in mind, he chose to educate his own sons at home. The relationship between him and Christie in particular seems to have been one of strong mutual influence, for he followed his son into both vegetarianism and, in 1906, the Esperanto movement, of which he became an enthusiastic advocate. Thomas Robinson was known to his grandchildren as Avo (Esperanto for 'grandfather'), and as late as 1917 he preached a sermon in Esperanto at Goodramgate Church in York.

Thomas Robinson died on 23rd May, 1923, aged 76. He and Maria spent the last years of his life living next door to Christie and his growing family in Kingston-upon-Thames in Surrey, and it was there that Thomas Robinson put the memoir of his time at Christ's Hospital into its final form. However, the account has its

INTRODUCTION

origins in the previous century, as a prefatory note written by Christie in 1959 makes clear:

> My father wrote this for a series of articles in a London magazine (now long extinct) called *The West End*. He altered the names of the masters concerned, to avoid possible legal proceedings, or pain to relatives.
>
> When he retired, he rewrote it enlarged, and with the correct names, and sometimes read extracts from it to Guido and me, when we were young, imitating the tone of voice of the speakers very skilfully.
>
> About three years ago I saw in a bookseller's circular an appeal from the Librarian of Christ's Hospital, asking for diaries or manuscripts about the period of this work, and I sent them my father's MS. They were very pleased to have it, as it filled a gap in the school history just between a previous and a subsequent date. They kept the MS (in a bulky volume), and made two copies in typewriting: one they kept, the other is this one.
>
> The earlier publication (in *The West End*) brought my father a number of letters from Old Boys who were delighted to have this account, and to confirm my father's experiences.

Thomas Robinson declines to give much background to the history of Christ's Hospital itself, but it may be helpful to mention that although Christ's Hospital is an old school, founded in the reign of Edward VI, it has always differed from other ancient independent schools in the extent to which it subsidises the fees of poorer pupils, and has traditionally drawn from a far wider social range. At the time Thomas Robinson attended, there were two schools for boys: one in Hertford for boys aged 7 to 9 (where the girls' school was also located), and one for older boys, in Newgate, London. The two parts of the memoirs deal with his time at the Hertford and London schools respectively.

Charlie Butler
April 2011

INTRODUCTION

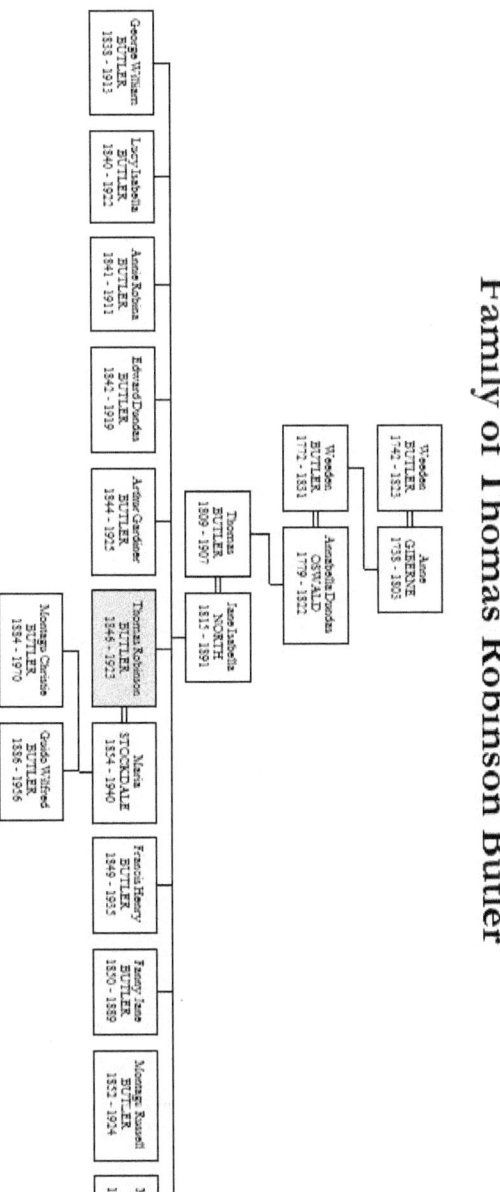

INTRODUCTION

CHRIST'S HOSPITAL, HERTFORD

RECOLLECTIONS
OF
CHRIST'S HOSPITAL

A TRUE ACCOUNT OF THE AUTHOR'S EXPERIENCES OF HIS
SCHOOLDAYS AT CHRIST'S HOSPITAL, HERTFORD FROM THE AGE
OF SEVEN TO NINE, AND AT CHRIST'S HOSPITAL, LONDON FROM
THE AGE OF NINE TO FIFTEEN.

BY THE REVD. T. R. BUTLER

January 19th, 1920

TOM BUTLER'S SCHOOLDAYS

CHRIST'S HOSPITAL, HERTFORD

THE HERTFORD SCHOOL (1853-55)

TOM BUTLER'S SCHOOLDAYS

HERTFORD WORDS

"Backs":	"I retract my agreement."
Bread, A:	A boy's allowance of bread
A brushing:	A flogging with the birch rod
Buck, A	Chief in fighting
A cake:	A cut on the hand with a cane
Chighky:	Glad
"Cross braces"	"I bear in mind that my braces are crossed." (The cross excused my lie)
Crug:	Crust
Doubler, A:	Two turns of the rope to one step
"Fin":	"I forbid"
"Fin backs":	"I forbid you to say backs"
"Go to bed, Tom"	Name of a certain rhythm in skipping
Have backs, To	To retract one's agreement
Housy:	Belonging to the inside of Christ's Hospital
Jolly:	Good, impressive, e.g. "A jolly sermon"
Keep the pot boiling, To:	To prevent cessation in long-rope Skipping
Luxent:	Delightful
On the sly:	To do a thing without anyone knowing
"Over to the left":	"I do not mean what I say"
To pole:	To disgrace as unclean
Poled:	In disgrace as polluted
Puncat, A:	One who tells tales of another
Puncat Day:	The 2nd of May, when punning is Allowed
Pun of, To:	To tell tales of
Shark, To:	To ask (for a piece)
Shoe, A:	A bread with crug on four sides
Skyblue:	Watered milk
Spicy words:	Long, grand words
Taffy, A:	A potato
Titch:	A caning on the tightened seat of the trousers

Touchy:	Rather
Towny:	Belonging to the outside of Christ's Hospital
Trade, A:	A food-service, e.g. a Breadboy, Pailboy, &c.
Turf:	A bread with crug on three sides
Woosent:	Very
Yellow, A:	A Yellow undercoat, worn in winter.

TOM BUTLER'S SCHOOLDAYS

Chapter 1. ENTRANCE

I have been asked to write an account of my recollections of Christ's Hospital. I was there from the age of 7 years 11 months until I become 15 years of age, and I am now 73, but though old, I am able to fulfil the request; for my memory is good and my desire is to write nothing but what is true. Can I trust my memory? Yes, for I can recollect correctly the names of all the numerous officials except one that I knew at Christ's Hospital, both at Hertford and at London, and there is no reason to think that my memory of other things is inaccurate. The exception is the clergyman of Hertford Church. I give no information of a guide-book character, such as the origin of the Foundation and the history of its Benefactors, for that does not belong to my personal experience as a Blue Coat boy at the School.

On the 2nd May, 1853, I was taken by my father to the Senior School, Christ's Hospital, Newgate Street, London, to be clothed in the Bluecoat dress and pass an educational examination by the head grammar school master, C.H. London, before going to the junior school, Christ's Hospital, Hertford. I put off "towny" clothes, underwent a medical examination, and put on "housy" ones. I put off a bright blue frock, over which, when it was returned home, my mother cried, and I put on a dark blue coat with leaden buttons, white bands, red girdle and yellow stockings. In winter-time a yellow coat called "a yellow" was worn underneath the blue coat, but only the front of the skirt of the yellow was seen. There was no covering for the head, except at the London School, and there it was only for a few minutes at an inspection. The city-arabs could not become reconciled to yellow stockings, and when they saw a bluecoat boy, were accustomed to call out to him, "Have you put your legs into the mustard-pot?"

The new boys, myself included, went, as we were led, from one place to another, until we were seated in a Hertford train. The journey seemed long. We were met by Mr Ludlow, the Steward of the Hertford School, who spoke as roughly to us as if he had known us for years. From Hertford Station we were marched into the Hall of the Foundation. Several of the lads, to whom discipline was new, were at once caned by Mr Hannum, the head Writing Master, who now entered, to superintend. I was in a terrible funk for I had never seen caning before, and I feared that this ogre would fly upon me. It greatly surprised me that he should wear the same kind of clothes as those worn by my father and family friends, silk hat and frock coat, and it occurred to me that possibly these garments might have a civilizing influence over him and at last conquer his savage nature.

We were then lodged in different wards, of which there were nine in the school at Hertford. I was placed in Ward 8, of which Mrs Meredith had charge. Over the door was painted, "No. VIII Ward, Nurse Meredith." There were at the time I entered about forty boys, most of them between seven and nine years old. They were just then having their supper, bread and butter and sky-blue (watered milk) the latter supplied from jacks (wooden pitchers).

The authorities of the School had given instructions to my father that I was to take a box with me of certain dimensions to as to fit easily into a hollow metal settle at the end of a Christ's Hospital bed. It cost fourteen shillings, and the sides are beautifully dove-tailed together. I have it now, and it is still useful to me. My father put into it for me the book *Robinson Crusoe*, which did not interest me, although I liked the true story on which it was founded, Alexander Selkirk.

The boys soon went to bed, and as the day had been a fatiguing one, I fell asleep long before the ringing of the curfew bell and the first cry of the watchman, which institutions were still observed as if they were as necessary as they used to be in former times.

TOM BUTLER'S SCHOOLDAYS

Chapter 2. THE WRITING SCHOOL

The sunbeams were playing upon the bed whereon I lay in Ward VIII and upon the garret-wall in front of me, when I opened my eyes the 3rd day of May, 1853, the first morning I spent in Christ's Hospital. How reproachful the sun is at this season, rising early, to a large mass of mankind! Scarcely awake I watched its dancing beams and was comfortable in their refreshing warmth, and filled with joy by their beauty. But suddenly the pleasing vision vanished. I looked around me and was painfully aware that I was not at home. Where am I? Then the events of yesterday flash across my mind, and joy takes its flight. Here I am to be for a long and dreary time and nothing can make things right till a period, the length of my life over again, is ended. There was no time to think the matter over. I got up at the sound of a bell, dressed in a certain set time, and during the first week of my life at School had my bed daily made for me by an older lad. I then went with others to the Writing School for an hour before breakfast.

The teaching at Christ's Hospital, Hertford, was conducted in two schools, one of them for English, reading writing, spelling and arithmetic, called The Writing School, the other for Latin and Greek grammar, called The Grammar School. At my examination on entering the Foundation I was considered to read and write fairly well for my early age. I was also able to decline the Latin nouns, musa, magister and dominus. Those new boys who at their examination upon entrance were found not to be able to read simple English, and sometimes were ignorant even of the English alphabet, were not allowed to go to the Grammar School. They had first to obtain sufficient English instruction to enable them to learn Latin. They therefore, morning and afternoon, attended the Writing School only, and it is obvious that to be too long in this backward condition and thus out of the Grammar School, was deemed disgrace for them. All the rest of the Christ's Hospital boys attended one of the two schools in the morning, and the other in the afternoon for a week, and in the following week reversed this order. As both Schools opened at the same hours through the day, it was necessary that four of the Wards – that is, half the boys of Christ's Hospital, should attend in reverse order to the other four wards. Thus all Christ's Hospital could be conveniently taught every day, and the morning instruction repeated in the afternoon. After an hour for breakfast in the Hall (described in the next chapter), I again went into the Writing School at nine o'clock, and was taught by Mr Sykes, the usher, until twelve. He was fifteen years old, and of an amiable disposition. He had just left Christ's Hospital, London, as a scholar there, and I saw him in the Bluecoat dress on the day that I put on my housy clothes in London.

Mr Sykes asked some questions but could scarcely obtain an answer. One child, being asked to spell a word, replied that he wished to return to his home; whereupon the usher smiled.

In this School we learnt by heart a selection of Psalms made from the Version of Sternhold and Hopkins.[1] These we sang in the Hall before our meals, also at "duty" (Prayers) in the Wards. At the bottom of one page of the book in the midst of a desolate space was the word "Satan" with a star. That was for ever a puzzle to me at Hertford, for the asterisk and its use was not explained. It is, I think, generally supposed to be known to a child by instinct. I can still recite from memory two verses of a very clever rendering of corresponding verses in the Bible, Psalm 104.

> "His chamber beams lie in the clouds full sure,
>   Which, as his chariots, are made him to bear;
> And there, with much swiftness, his course doth endure,
>   Upon the wings riding of wind in the air.
> He maketh his spirits as heralds to go,
>   And lightnings to serve we see also prest,
> His will to accomplish they run to and fro,
>   To save or consume things, as seemeth Him best."

I have already said that the head master here was Mr Hannum. The expression of his face was that of one who suffered mental agonies on account of injuries committed on him by others; his look was austere and sour, and a smile did not become him, for it was mixed up with a frown. To the other masters he was scarcely civil, and they could not like him: one of them quarrelled with him and left. Daily he would show off his authority by suddenly bawling out, "Stop the School." The clamour of voices ceased and everyone listened, knowing what would follow. He then said, "Time is precious, go on again." But occasionally

---

[1] Thomas Sternhold's and John Hopkins' metrical psalter dates from 1549, but was decidedly old-fashioned by the nineteenth century.

Mr Hannum forgot to do this, and all would miss it, and say, Why is this? Mr Hannum has not said "Stop the School, time is precious, go on again." But one day there was a second "Stop the School!" There was a gentleman with him, a visitor. "What?" thought I, "is he going to show to this gentleman also the value of time?" I was wrong. He said, "This gentleman has kindly asked me to give each one of you, from him, two pence: and the money will now be distributed, and I thank him on your behalf."

None of the masters in the Writing School used the cane but Mr Hannum; each of them sent those of his scholars who were to be punished to a certain post and about every twenty minutes the head master came to the post to see if there were any culprits there, and if there were, asked no questions and exercised his privilege, giving two cuts each with the cane, aiming at the tips of the fingers.

Another master was Mr Hill who instructed me when I had done with the usher. Here I was employed in teaching a boy who was about two years older than myself. He asked me if I did not think the alphabet very difficult. I replied, "Everything is difficult to one who does not know it, but when you do know the alphabet, it would not seem difficult to you any longer." This, I said to encourage him, for he was anxious to learn. The Greek alphabet is easier to learn than the English at Christ's Hospital, for the Blues have a rhyme to help them with it. Alpha, Beta, Gamma, Delta, Knock a woman down and pelt her; Epsilon, Zeta, Heta, Theta, Pick her up again and beat her.

Mr Hill was a very tall man with an extremely small head. His happiness seemed to consist chiefly in endeavouring to make his scholars do justice to the commas, colons and semi-colons in their reading; so much so, that when one failed in his efforts, the fault was resented by the master as if the offender had done him some mean and cowardly injury. Every day he sent several to be caned on this account. But Mr Hill had amiable qualities. One on occasion I made a large blot in my copybook; this being overlooked, his attention was called to it by a little lad next to me; whereupon he excused me, and soundly boxed the lad's ears. He used sometimes to talk of taking us for an excursion. The treat was never realised, but it was kind of him to think of it.

CHRIST'S HOSPITAL, HERTFORD

Chapter 3. BREAKFAST

At eight o'clock a.m., a bell rang for breakfast, and we went into the Hall. Here there was a long table and forms for every ward, nine tables in all, for about 40 boys each, and there was also a platform in front containing a table and chair for Mr Ludlow, the Steward. Mr Ludlow was short and stout, wore spectacles, had a red face, and his cheeks moved continually after the manner of a pair of bellows. He had a magisterial authority over the boys, and every complaint was referred to him. Just now he held a wooden hammer, with which he solemnly struck the table. This action was a signal for the singers who led the psalm in "duty" (prayers) to go to their places, and for the reader of the service to ascend the pulpit. The words of the Psalms to be sung were a selection from Sternhold and Hopkins, and were learnt by heart in the Writing School. The tunes were taught to the boys at convenient times in the Hall by Mr Crossman, one of the Beadles. He knew the tunes and their pitches by ear and recollection, and used no instrument.

After duty, the "trades" who were the Bread-boys, Butter-boys, Milk-boys, Knife-boys, now brought up from the Kitchen large and small baskets and pails for the several Wards. These contained "breads" - pieces of bread each of the same size for every boy, pats of butter, milk and scalding water, knives, wooden spoons and bowls. These things were brought to each Ward by the trades of that Ward. If a bread had two "crugs" (crusts), one, top, the other, bottom, there was no special name for it, it was merely a "bread"; if it had three crugs, it was a "turf" and valued, and if it had four crugs, crust over four of the six sides, it was a "shoe" and very much valued. The lad to whom a shoe was laid felt grateful to the Bread-boy who favoured him with it. In the oven there were slight depressed lines formed by adjoining bricks. These produced the appearance of a cane on the bread baked upon them. A bread with a cane on it was thought unlucky, and I have seen a child shed tears, and implore the breadboy to give him another bread instead. The breadboy replied, "I'm sorry, I can't, I must lay it to someone."

The sign of the cane did not trouble me for I was not superstitious. As to the quality of the bread, unhappily its flavour was not like that of the "luxent" (enjoyable) bread sold in the shops outside. Some of the breads contained cockroaches, and the search for them was not always successful. When not so, one's two middle upper teeth felt something slippery resisting their pressure. This was the thin but strong coat of a cockroach, and the teeth were set on edge. Once, only once, in my experience, a boy found a mouse in his bread. He took it to Mr Ludlow, thinking this the proper thing to do. Mr Ludlow, however, was waxy, and expressing no sorrow on account of the shocking death of late Mr Mouse, nor any pity for the poor hungry child before him, said testily, "I didn't make the bread, what do you come to me for?"

The boys often converted their butter into curd. The process took away its rankness, but left in it very little taste. They beat together for some time, with a wooden spoon, a fair amount of wet crumbled crumb and their butter, until the substance became a sticky greasy stodge. They then diluted it with milk and water. The curd rose to the surface of the liquid in the bowl, and was taken off and eaten with the dry bread left.

During breakfast the children consulted their "fairies" as to their luck for the day. The fairies were glass bead rings of various colours which they wore on their fingers. The beads were counted according to some method, which I forget, to words, "Fairy, fairy, conjure me to have letters from home today", or "Fairy, fairy, conjure me not to be caned by Mr Keymer", or similarly to other requests. If the sign were not propitious, the child sometimes smacked his ring to punish the fairy. We did not all believe in these charms but liked to wear them as ornaments and consult them for amusement, and thus follow fashion.

Mr Ludlow now walked about the Hall to enquire from the Nurse of every Ward whether she had any reports to make of bad behaviour among the boys. If she had, the transgressors were stationed at the Steward's table to be caned by him after the Wards had been dismissed. The two monitors of each Ward also could make a report, like to the Nurse's, but they seldom did so. Other boys did not "pun of" (tell tales of) one another, for if one did, he was called a "puncat". The exceptional puncat was listened to, however, without disgust, by Mr Ludlow. M., whose parents had not taught him how to pronounce and spell the word *indecent*, walked up to him, and complained, "Please, Sir, N. has said an *undecent* word." This outrage on the English language had an exceeding interest for Mr Ludlow, who was a very important and dignified man, while N.'s offence, to all appearances, had no interest. However, I think that N. received two cuts of the cane when the Hall had cleared. It was a proud moment for Mr

CHRIST'S HOSPITAL, HERTFORD

Ludlow. "Undecent?" shouted he, in a shocked magisterial voice, and all the Hall was called to attention. In pompous words he related the present abuse of language, and proclaimed its correction for the benefit of the whole assembly of boys and nurses, and gave a sententious harangue on the duty of Christ's Hospital to speak good English.

But as to punning, the 2nd of May was, with the Hertford boys, different from every other day in the year. "The second of May is Puncat day." On the 2nd of May, it was well understood, every one might pun of another. Mr Ludlow did not know this. He listened to the first puncat, but when a crowd came to his table with tales, some true and some invented, he got furious and slashed them away with his cane.

The routine of breakfast being over, Mr Ludlow dismissed the Wards in order, and then caned those who stood near his table to be punished. Among these there were sometimes foolish little asses who had stationed themselves there voluntarily. They wished their companions, who waited below, to admire them as heroes for their fortitude in bearing pain. All of these youngsters descended the Hall staircase smiling, though some of them were unable to refrain from tears. Occasionally Mr Ludlow was absent from Hall at breakfast-time. In that case, Mr Hill, a Writing Schoolmaster, was his substitute as Steward. He used to have his breakfast brought to him, two eggs, bread, butter and coffee. After he had eaten half of his meal, he called up the Steward's table a certain boy who was a relation to him, and gave him the other half. "Why does Mr Hill eat his breakfast before us?" said a boy to me. "Probably because he has no time to eat it at home." "Do you think," suggested the boy, "that he wants to make us lash?" "Certainly not," I replied, "what could he do more than give half away to one of us? It is very kind of him!"

Chapter 4. No. VIII WARD

The new clothes were very difficult for a new boy of the age of seven to button and unbutton. New leaden buttons were awkwardly tight in their stiff holes for weak little fingers to undo. If a child of that age agreed to pay twopence to an older lad to button and unbutton his clothing for him during dressing in the morning, undressing in the evening, and at any other time necessary, the nurse allowed this arrangement for the newcomer's first week. I myself was ashamed to be, like a babe, unable to dress and undress, and therefore managed somehow without help, but with great difficulty.

Letters home were read by the Nurse. All the Ward had to place their letters open at a window-sill for her to read. This did not seem fair, but, however, we thought that it did not much matter what we wrote to long as we put in the words, "Mrs Meredith is very kind to us." I could say this with truth, for she favoured me more than others on account of my gentle manners and appearance and because I gave her no trouble. After a time it occurred to me that I might write and post my letters "on the sly".

In her best mood Mrs Meredith was a well meaning woman. She performed cheerfully the ordinary work of a nurse, looking after a whole Ward of children, which was necessarily a heavy business. She seemed to enjoy tubbing the smaller boys, using soft, yellow, almost liquid soap, the same which the charwoman used for cleaning the Ward floor. In a quick business-like way she washed the heads and backs of the bigger boys which were held over wooden vats. She taught the Ward how to part their hair with a brush, and to save the trouble of using a comb, so that the latter soon became of no use. She supplied from the palms of her hands to every head a liberal quantity of oil, and one had to be careful that it did not travel to his bands. Sometimes she was good-humoured and at other times solemn. When good humoured she told us of a conversation she once had with Princess Victoria, afterwards Queen. She mistook the Princess for a dress-maker but discovered the mistake after parting from her. When solemn, Mrs Meredith sermonised to the boys: "It is wicked," said she, "to do wrong, and those who are wicked come to a bad end. Telling lies leads to stealing, and stealing to murder, and then you are hanged. Suppose you should be struck dead this instant, where would you go? Where would those boys go whom I had to scold this morning? They must first turn over a new leaf, and if they don't, I shall tell Mr Ludlow of them."

It was fortunate for me that Mrs Meredith liked me. On one occasion she favoured me at the supper table before all the Ward. She brought to me a plateful of fruit pie out of her private room. I thought for a moment it must have come from home, but could not think how. On another day she showed that, to a boy who offended her, she could be spiteful. She took the cake, which had been sent to him from home, out of the Ward cupboard, cut it up into about forty pieces, and distributed them in the Ward. "What a shame!" said we in an undertone one to another, but poor wretches, we were half-starving and in a few moments the whole large cake was devoured, not one of us having the grace to refuse. To another little wretch who committed a transgression, which he could not help, but which gave her trouble, she showed a violence and vindictiveness of a fury, without having the sense of justice which is attributed to that mythological character. I shall never forget the sound of the scuffling, banging and fierce words "I'll teach you" which I heard outside the garret where we slept; it was the harsh treatment of a child scarcely more than an infant. The words "I'll teach you" are probably as old as the time of Gideon, for it is said of him that he "taught the men of Succoth". I thought of the Nurse afterwards when I heard a man who was whacking a frog say to it, "I'll teach you to be a frog".

On entering Ward VIII the children soon made one another's acquaintance. Three of the lads who made friends with me were Leggate, Sanders and Morrison. Morrison showed me a large Noah's Ark, which was given to him by Redpath, a Christ's Hospital Governor. Sanders taught me to count from one to twenty in Welsh. Leggate, a lame lad, who walked by the help of a crutch, had a great affection for me. I had to be very careful not to offend him, for he carried a sharp wooden dagger, and was inclined to be passionate. Once momentarily forgetting his friendship, he made a hole in my face with his dagger. "What's the matter with your cheek?" called to me the Nurse who saw the wound and blood trickling from it. Now I knew that Leggate was not master of his temper, so I said that the trouble was not intended. Leggate, echoing my words, said, "It was my doing, and not intended; it was an accident." "Leggate," said she, "you must be more careful." He was exceedingly sorry, and I forgave him. The lads of our Ward, finding that I knew how to use a needle, and had in my box the suitable material to keep it employed, requested me to make bags for their marbles. I sold the bags to them a penny each, and soon made a gratifying little sum. These little ones did not bully one another for they were too much of an age, but they were, on account of their equality, able to defend themselves and were as pugnacious as bantams. The best fighter was called "buck of the Ward". They were, however, as a rule very friendly with another through sleeping in one garret, telling invented fairy stories, or listening to them, till they fell asleep.

Another item of interest in Ward-life, which amused me on account of its absurdity, was that everyone, whatever his condition in health, was obliged to go once a month to the Sick Ward to drink a small cupful of jalap, strong enough for a man of fifty. I usually, if I could, kept the large dose in my mouth till I got into the playground, where I spat it out. The poor lads were always hungry. Some would beg for orange peel and even pick it up from the sandy Ward floor, make it clean, and devour it. Others bartered the food of the day for that of the day following by the rule, "Two crugs tomorrow for one crug today," so that, sitting down to a meal, there were those who had almost nothing at all. I saw the folly of this bartering and its injustice. I was, however, terribly hungry and especially at night. Once I had a dream like that of the "hungry man" in Isaiah, who "dreameth, and behold, he eateth; but he awaketh, and his soul is empty." I thought I had under my pillow six towny rolls, but awaking, searched for them in vain. Cold and hunger, caused by want of nourishing food, gave us various complaints. All the tips of my fingers festered, and were full of yellow pus, and a thumbnail came off; my eyelids stuck together in my sleep and when I opened my eyes several lashes came out. One day a young lady of about 18, whom I had never seen before, and have never seen since, took me outside the Hospital, bought me a paper-bagful of confectionery, and then brought me again to my Ward. She was some kind of cousin. I was disappointed, for the affair did not last more than about a quarter of an hour. I thought it over, and concluded that she had made a promise to call upon me, and had thus fulfilled it. After I had been in the Ward some little time, I was made a Monitor of it but was considered by the Nurse too lenient. I did not knock about the noisy boys; they liked me, but were not afraid of me. I, however, opposed the Buck of the Ward whom they disliked, and they put him into Coventry.

CHRIST'S HOSPITAL, HERTFORD

Chapter 5. DINNER

After morning school was over, there was an hour to spend before dinner, either in the playground or in the Ward, and then the Hall bell rang twice, and all the scholars and Nurses ascended the Hall-staircase for the midday meal. As we were ascending, I heard Mrs Graham of No. VII Ward and Mrs Meredith of No. VIII Ward talking and laughing about my hair. It was very long, and in time past at my home had been curled with curling-tongs, and in a day or two would have to be cut short. I myself had no objection to part with my curls, but I did feel grieved when, on Sunday Evening, the girls of the Bluecoats Girls' School close by, came into the Hall, and I saw that their heads had been cropped like those of the boys. When we were all seated, Mr Ludlow, the Steward, gave the same three solemn taps on this table for "duty" before the meal (a psalm and prayers) as in the morning. After duty, which lasted about quarter of an hour, the "trades", meatboys, pailboys, &c. brought up from the Kitchen hollow platters, containing boiling water inside, and meat upon them, and, in the pails, taffies, cooked in their skins, also knives and two-pronged forks. Mr Ludlow, during dinner, walked about the Hall, and if any Nurse or boy wished to speak to him, now was the opportunity. A lad, for example, complained to him that the meat was high. Mr Ludlow tasted it, spat it out of his mouth, and said it was very good.

After dinner at a separate table, beer was given to delicate boys, of whom I was one. In old-fashioned times beer was believed to convey strength just as nowadays meat is supposed to give it. And indeed for those poor little wretches, whatever may be said now, a stimulant seemed to be necessary. "Give strong drink, says King Lemuel, unto him that is ready to perish, and wine unto the bitter in soul." A small mug of sweet ale was a slight comfort to such a one, and did him no harm. When the beer was flat and sharp, it was a disappointment. Flesh is also a stimulant. There was always in each Ward one boy who got nothing of it, and that was the unfortunate to whom was laid the bladebone. No one ate the bladebone, or what was on it, for it was considered unclean. If one ate it in ignorance, he was "poled" (polluted) and no boy spoke to him.

The children were very superstitious but, after all, not more so than many grown-ups of the present time. It was thought lawful to tell a lie if one did but cross something – it mattered not what. It was sufficient to remember that one's braces were crossed and to say to oneself, "Cross braces." The belief was held that everyone dies from slow poisoning. For all food, said they, contains poison except carrots, and gradually produces death. And it would be of no avail to eat nothing but carrots, even if one could do so, for then death by starvation would follow, carrots not having by themselves sufficient nourishment to preserve life.

Dinner was followed by after-meal duty, and then we were dismissed or occasionally detained to witness a brushing in public. That is a flogging with a birch-rod on the bare back of some sinful boy. The culprit was hung on the back of a beadle, and another beadle furrowed the flesh with the rod. For example, Mr Ludlow, to his credit, hated cruelty to dumb animals, and sentenced a boy, who had set light to the fur of a cat's back, to be birched once a month. We all agreed that the boy deserved to be brushed, but thought that once a month was too much, and not right because it looked more like revenge than punishment. However, after one brushing, I think the matter ended. During a brushing if the one who was chastised groaned from excessive pain, the boys who witnessed involuntarily cried "shame". The beadle in pity gave less vigorous strokes. Then Mr Ludlow called to him, "Do your duty, Sir," and if the beadle became loath, took the rod out of the beadle's hand and administered the strokes himself.

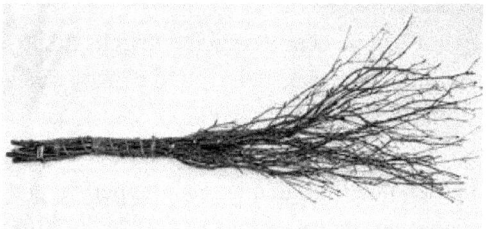

The birch is quite different from a cane, and designed to break the skin

After dinner, Mr Crossman, one of these beadles, was employed in taking those whose turn it was outside the foundation for a walk until the school hour. There were two walks which were convenient for him, and we always went on either one or the other of them. At this time it was usual for someone to ask him to foretell the weather, for all of us knew that he was proud of his supposed ability to do this. "Halt!," shouted he in military style. We all stood still and he, with an air of importance, gazed at the sky for some seconds and then proclaimed what the weather would be. It was the duty of Mr Crossman nightly to walk about Christ's Hospital with a bell and a dog and at each half hour to proclaim loudly the time of night. The boys imagined that he guarded the Hospital from highwaymen, and sometimes it was rumoured that he had shot one of them. The boys greatly admired this faithful beadle's valour and bore no ill will against him because he was employed by Mr Ludlow to do the birching. He was a kind-hearted man and evidently did not like that business, for it was horribly cruel and especially for young children.

There was a shop in one of the playgrounds which was kept by Mr Allen, a very stout man. He was a beadle, but not liked as Mr Crossman was, for he took no interest in the children, was irritable and devoid of humour. The scholars were obliged to buy from his shop, for there was no other. Nothing was allowed to be bought outside the school, and housy coin alone was permitted, the sixpence of which was copper and in shape a hexagon. Mr Ludlow, if he could, prevented any boy from possessing more than a shilling. The surplus was delivered to the Nurse of that boy's Ward.

Unfortunately Mr Ludlow also had no sense of humour. A child, sent by his companions to the shop for some "pigeon's milk" was reported to the Steward, and mercilessly punished. Another lad requested Mrs Allen to sell him a pennyworth of what she hadn't got: whereupon Mr Allen rose in great anger to seize him. The little boy got fairly away, but the fat man fell forward over the door-step, and was laid up for some time. The children of Christ's Hospital did not pity him and regarded his accident as a punishment for his stupidity.

The Hertford Christ's Hospital boys were very respectful to their Nurses; yet when by themselves in the playgrounds, had many a merry laugh about the Nurses' supposed unsuccessful attempts to talk like ladies and educated persons. I think this is interesting, for it shows how observant are even little children scarcely out of infancy. They told anecdotes to one another about their Nurses' use of "spicy" words. Spicy with them meant long or grand. Thus, <u>combatant</u> is the spicy word for <u>fighter</u>. They were never tired of the following story which they believed to be true. A Nurse reported to the Steward a fight. "Oh, Sir, when I was on my perambulations, I saw two combatants combating, and if I hadn't contifered, I don't know what would have been the insequences!"

This story was followed by another with the preface, "Don't believe this that I am going to tell you, I think it was made up by some boy, but what I said before is true:- A Nurse said once, 'It isn't the walue of the thing, nor do it magnify, but I won't be composed upon.'"

CHAPTER 6. GAMES

The Head Master of the Grammar School was the Reverend Nathaniel Keymer. Those of his scholars who had not been to him in the morning, but whose turn it was, according to the school plan for attendance described in Chapter 2, to go to him in the afternoon, came, as soon as they were released from the Writing School, to the door of the Grammar School, to enquire what was the Keymer news.

"Did Mr Keymer look as if he would be kind this afternoon?" "How many raps did he give?" "How many titches?" "How many cakes?" "Did Natty Keymer (his son) come from London to put him in a good humour?" These questions were anticipated by Mr Keymer's morning classes, and the answers were accordingly got ready. There was not much sense, if any, in the questions and answer, for whatever the answer might be, the effect on the mind was always terror. But that could not be helped: the air of Christ's Hospital was not favourable to the reasoning faculty. If the report of the morning was bad, there was nothing good to be expected in the afternoon; if, on the other hand, it was good, the scholars thought that Mr Keymer's better temper than usual was only temporary, and therefore not for the afternoon, and this also was very alarming. There was nothing to be done to relieve the mind of these scholars, who were going to Mr Keymer in the afternoon, but to derive what consolation they could from the thought that the time had not yet come. The dinner hour intervened, and after that, about three-quarters of an hour. If, as they hoped much, dinner should take up less time than usual, there would be a precious hour of even an hour and a quarter before their misery came to pass. They must after dinner make the time appear to go as slowly as possible, and this the children conceived they could do by constantly looking at the clock.

I think that the boys of Hertford were more fond of play and more spirited, and indeed more like boys than the lads of London. The reason was partly that on arrival at London their spirit was knocked out of them by the bullying of the bigger boys, and partly that the boys of Hertford were more favoured in their games than those of London by the possession of a field. Thus the Hertford boys were able to play cricket, whereas in London the scholars had to content themselves with the less manly game of rounders.

On a very hot day, however, when much running about is more a toil than a pleasure, the quiet amusement of Yards was very popular for the children to play in the field. It suited their childish fancy for it was a game of pretence. A portion of the field was marked out with string for an imaginary palace. This was sub-divided into a royal apartment for a sultan and his court to lounge in, and other apartments, which were for slaves. In order to get a comfortable lounge for the royal apartment, a great deal of grass was collected. Slaves were sent all over the field to barter for grass. The conditions of barter were sung to one C, followed by a downward cadence B, A, G, the time, tones and words being as follows: -

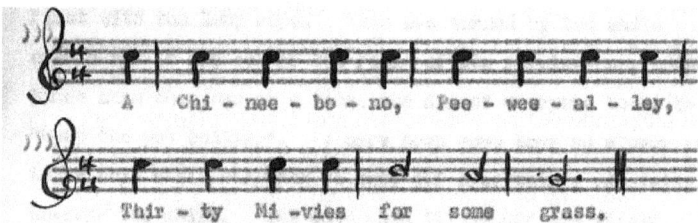

A Chi - nee - bo - no, Pee - wee - al - ley,
Thir - ty Mi - vies for some grass.

and, as each slave instinctively waited to commence his song at a suitable point of time, the effect over the field was that of weird round which was evidently enjoyed. One or two slaves were also sent to the shop to buy refreshments for the Sultan and his court, biscuits, sweets, sherbet, &c. When all the slaves had returned with their grass and refreshments to the Sultan, they settled in their own apartments in the palace, and had pieces of biscuit thrown to them over the string which divided them from the Sultan and his friends, who were reclining on mounds of grass, eating and drinking. Whether or not any sherbet was handed over to the slaves I forget. The expenses were paid by the Sultan and his court.

Other games of these little ones were Blindman's buff, Hop-scotch, Knucklebones, Marbles, Oranges & Lemons, School, and Skipping. A few of the children were very cruel to animals. They amused themselves by beheading beetles, which they called "soldiers and sailors", and by "taming flies" - cutting their wings off and making the insects walk with pins stuck through them. I said to one of the young demons, "How would you like a giant, such as we read of in fairy tales, to make you walk with a great spike thrust through your body?" They never hurt a spider for they would have thought it unlucky to do so. Of one thing I feel sure; it is no superstition. It is unlucky to be really cruel to any living thing.

In Skipping, the Hertford children were very expert. First with the long rope. This was turned by two while others ran in and out of the field of its revolutions, sometimes more than one at a time, the aim of everyone being to "keep the pot boiling". I have seen some boys so clever as to be able while skipping to take off everything, retaining however the shirt. The coat when it was off was wisely rolled up before it was pitched away: the boots, breeches and stocking were more difficult to take off. Secondly with a short rope, turned by the skipper. Sometimes he crossed his arms and afterwards recrossed them. Sometimes he kept up the simple step for hundreds of turns; I have seen the number reach a thousand; sometimes many doublers were performed. A double was two turns of the rope to one step. My greatest number of doublers was forty-six, but some boys attained to many more. A very favourite recreation in skipping and not difficult for those who were fairly good skippers was the rhythm called "Go to Bed, Tom". Doubler, single, doubler, single, doubler, doubler, doubler, single.

One day when I was in the playground in front of Ward VIII where I used to skip, a gentleman walked into it from outside Christ's Hospital. He was very kindly and was pleased to talk to the boys, and we gathered together in front of him. He discoursed to us about the moon, and this is the substance of what he said:- "Now, my boys, you often look at the moon, but I dare say you think nothing about it. The people who live in the moon call this world their moon, but what we call our moon they call their earth. Some silly persons say there are no people in the moon. I dare say that some persons in the moon think that there are no people here. But how they would laugh if we could only tell them what some persons say here! Why, this earth is their moon. Are there not people here?- ("Yes, Sir" – "No, Sir" – "Yes, Sir") – There are; and, of course, there are people in the moon as well. I cannot answer all the questions you might put to me about them, as I don't know everything. Well, yes, yes; I don't know everything; nobody knows everything. But they are just as curious to know all about us as we are to know about them. I suppose you know that this world and the moon revolve round each other. Ah! If you take pains, you will, when you get older, learn a great many things which you do not know now. Even I can always learn something fresh."

One day in the year the Governors of Christ's Hospital came into the field and showered all sorts of eatables for which the children scrambled, lobsters, pork pies, oranges, cakes and what not; also a great many halfpence. I never approved of scrambling, and I did not enter into it then, for I regarded it as ill-mannered. I noticed that the roughest and rudest of the boys got almost everything. When all was over I searched the ground and found a halfpenny concealed in the grass. "How very kind of these rich men" thought I, "to spend such large sums of money as they must have spent, to buy all these good things for us, poor half-starving children! But what a pity it is that they have not the sense to perceive that the scramble is no treat at all to many of us, but only a disappointment! What shocking bad taste these rich Governors of Christ's Hospital have! They ought to know that Christ and his apostles, though poor men, were gentlemen, and have left us instructions in good manners. Yet in spite of all the New Testament teaching on the subject, the Governors of this Foundation called by His Name encourage the roughness and rudeness of those who were so unfortunate as to be ill bred by their parents, and are scarcely responsible."

What struck me as remarkable was that these rich men took a strange pleasure in the selfish low scuffle they caused for the things they threw. I was not angry with the poor hungry lads who got fed, for they acted according to their natural instinct. Like fowls in a barn-yard, they snatched their prizes, pushed, and kicked all who were near them. I was very glad that they were fed. What I thought was, "What is the gain of a lobster or a large pork pie, if, in order to obtain it, gentility must be renounced, and one's self-respect lost?"

I did once when I was very hungry obtain something to eat in a way that I do not approve of now. It did not occur to me that I was encouraging a vicious spirit. I received a penny from a boy who could spare it in return for the pleasure I gave him by allowing him to give me six cuts with the cane, three cuts on each hand.

I have said nothing yet about the game of marbles, but there is really nothing worth saying, excepting that the Hertford children were very expert at it. When they removed to London they soon lost much of their skill. I recall the past as if it were the present. A boy suddenly stops in the middle of the game and will play no more. The others naturally ask, "Where are you going?" He then answers, "It is half past one, and I have go to Mr Keymer this afternoon." "What has he gone for?" is now asked. "He has gone to funk for Mr Keymer before the clock." "Is it so late? I must go too."

Their hearts beat more and more painfully as the time draws nearer, and at last the terrible bell rings. They hear the last three or four dying sounds, and then, gaining resolution from necessity, enter the Grammar School. At this time they have always compared themselves to sheep going to a slaughter-house; and indeed I suppose that the sheep cannot be more nervous.

Chapter 7. THE GRAMMAR SCHOOL

There were three masters in the Grammar School, the Revd. Nathaniel Keymer, the Revd. Henry Hawkins and Mr Bowry, who took the lowest classes. Mr Bowry was a bulky and dangerous-looking man, and very bearish in his ways towards the poor little kiddies under him. He made unsparing and senseless use of the cane in order to make them learn and recollect the parts of speech in the Latin Grammar, which was to them, and perhaps to him, unintelligible jargon. The Latin Grammar appeared to me, at my early age, probably the composition of a lunatic, not so much on account of the names of the cases, Nominative, Genitive, Dative, etc., which to me seemed to be as nonsensical as High, diddle, diddle; Fiddle-de-dee; Dickory dickory dock; but because of the English in the declension of <u>lapis</u> a stone. Take the words "O stone." "What sane man," thought I, "would ever think of speaking to a stone?" I was however pleased with the sentences, <u>Tempus fugit</u>, time flies, and <u>Magister docet</u>, the master teaches. When afterwards under another master I learnt the Greek Grammar, I was pleased with the musical sound of the declension of <u>Keras</u>, a horn, and its contractions.

When out of school, the boys sometimes saw Mr Bowry walking with his little girl and would not have exchanged with her for worlds.

After a short time Mr Hawkins became my master. He was not coarse in manner and appearance and speech like the former master, and on the first morning after the holidays graciously condescended to say "Good morning" to his scholars. I chiefly recollect him as frequently flapping his arms and gown as if he were imitating a barn fowl when it lifts itself up on its legs and flaps vigorously. This process was to fan the room, and it became a constant habit. Mr Hawkins, by way of punishment, gave a great many titches, that is, canings on the seat of the trousers pulled tight over the form. Occasionally he gave a brushing (birching). Selecting one of the lads, he would cross-examine him upon some trifle in such a manner that the scholar would, through nervousness, unwittingly contradict himself and apparently tell a lie. Then the guilty one was strapped to a form, and brushed for several minutes, Mr Hawkins, throughout the performance, loudly bewailing his hard lot in having so painful a duty to perform.

CHRIST'S HOSPITAL, HERTFORD

On one occasion myself and another were each separately questioned on a certain matter; but I never knew what it was. Mr Hawkins easily discovered incongruity and settled that he would victimise the older of us. I was then eight, and the other, luckily for me, had turned nine. He was brushed, and I got off with merely six cakes (cuts on the hand with the cane).

I remained with Mr Hawkins some months, and was then removed to the Rev. Nathaniel Keymer. This master had a fine aquiline nose, long face and chin, a mouth curved downwards, expressing the reverse of a smile, and long hair waving concavely and gracefully below the neck. He wore, at all times, a tall silk hat on the back of his head, his eyes were gravely turned as he spoke, and he jerked out his words with little nods. His study had a window through which he would see his two classes outside, and they could see his nose refracted in the panes and distorted.

Mr Keymer's pronunciation of English was very remarkable. In his use of a vowel he conformed to no recognised sound, it was merely a link between consonants so that only about two vowel sounds were usually required. What was the reason of this? Had he any scheme to simplify English? No, at that time, so far as I know, the idea of improving English had not occurred to anyone. Of course, in singing, one is allowed to change a vowel if that given in a dictionary is impossible. Try to sing <u>pip</u> in a long-continued tone. You will find that you cannot do it; you must therefore sing <u>peep</u> instead. But that is another matter. If Mr Keymer's pronunciation cannot be explained, I must leave it unexplained. There are strange things in the world which are a puzzle to all men, the scientific world included. For example, musk, since 1902, has lost its scent.[2] Why? No one knows. I suggest that perhaps Mr Keymer was vowel-deaf. If that idea seems feasible to the reader, I will suppose that perhaps <u>did</u> and <u>dud</u> sounded exactly the same on the drum of his ear, just as in a similar way <u>green</u> and <u>red</u> have the same appearance to a man that is colour-blind. As to the word <u>you</u>, Mr Keymer sometimes pronounced it <u>yer</u>, sometimes <u>yo</u>, and sometimes <u>yow</u>. When he passed his classes, he said, "Mannit, Mannit, Mannit". Mannit

---

[2] "Mr. Thomas Wilkinson, a native of Lancashire, now a Fifeshire farmer, some sixty years ago began growing musk for the Liverpool market. He soon had a monopoly of the trade and sold 5,000 plants a week during the months of May. In 1898, he stated, he noticed the plants began to acquire a rank, leafy smell, and at the end of the summer he sold his business. Four years later he returned to Liverpool and found the musk plants then on sale scentless." Eric Hardy, Letter to the Editor, *Nature* (1 September 1934), p.327,

meant Minute. It was an abbreviated form of the sentence "I shall hear your lesson in a minute," and the repetition was doubtless for emphasis. Another abbreviation was "Lasson, Lasson, Lasson". It was the repetition of the sentence, "Learn your lesson" and was an alteration or variation of the monotony of "Mannit". These sentence words, at the rate of one to a step or second, appeared to be spoken subconsciously and from force of habit. Mr Keymer's common way of expressing his displeasure was to call his scholars "cats and pags", that is, cats and pigs.

The Latin lesson was generally the same - "the parts of speech to the end of <u>Audior</u>". This took up a long time. Mr Keymer standing with one foot on the form before the boys, the other on the ground, moved round to every one to hear him in turn say his part. In one hand Mr Keymer held a cane, in the other the wrist of the lad whose turn it was to speak. The master was thus ready to deal at once with a mistake, and to chastise the delay of an instant. He twisted the poor child's wrist backwards and forwards, rapping meanwhile the back and front of the little one's hand so that the child in excruciating pain stood with difficulty on one leg and sometimes fell. One day one of the scholars failing to say his lesson correctly, the master addressed him thus: "Has your Ward got a cat?" "Yes, Sir." "Just brang that cat tomorrow to scole with yo, and evry word yer don't know, just ask that cat. Shay'll tell yo! O yes! Shay'll tell yo. I'm perfectly sartin that a cat would say its lassons better than yow doe."
Occasionally a boy forgot to bring one of his books to school with him. "I know the rayson," said Mr Keymer, "why yo dadn't brang that book. Yer thought the book might come by itself. Of course the book can walk about just the same as yow. Or yer thought yer wouldn't take the trouble to brang it. Yer'd tell mey to go and fetch it for yo. That was it, I know. Yer thank that if yo want anything, avrybody must go and gat it anstantly. Yer thought yow old just tell the first person yer met to go and fetch it for yo. I'm sure that was the rayson." Then addressing the class, "I navver dad say such a parcel of filthy cats and pags in my whole life. It makes me sack to say yo."

The long lesson being at last finished, the children are glad to walk to the benches outside the study, and plan all sorts of tortures to inflict upon their master when they are grown up.[3]

---

[3] In fact, Rev. Keymer suffered complete a mental breakdown shortly after retirement to the living of Colne

CHRIST'S HOSPITAL, HERTFORD

CHAPTER 8. INSTRUCTION ON THE CHRISTIAN RELIGION

On Saturday Mr Keymer gave instruction on the <u>Christian religion</u>. The class being assembled in his study, he read the usual prayer, and immediately, without a pause, called out "Yo dadn't bow", instantly caning some little boy whom he had noticed. Throughout the caning he thus reproached the innocent one for his refusal to abuse Holy Scripture: "Yer don't thank it worth the trouble to boy yo'er head, do yer? All Chrastians bow their head. But they may do what they like for what yow care. Oh no! Yo'er not a Chrastian, yer don't care about it. The Scrapture say, 'Avry kney <u>shall</u> bow', but I might was well talk to a haythen as to yo." He then commenced his lesson to the class, who stood behind a line of forms in his study. He was holding his cane in his hand. "Now aych of yow are to repate after may what I am going to tell yo. Yow began, Her bayganneth the first chapter of the Holy Gospel according tow Saint John." "Here beginneth." "Now go on – I can't have yer stopping." "Please Sir, Here beginneth the first Epistle of the Gospel of St Job." "It asn't, it asn't. Mind if yow say that again, I'll gave yo the barch rod." "Next boy, repate. The annunciation of the blassed Vargin Mary." "The annuncication of the Virgin Mary." "I didn't say that. Now mind, I won't have you layving out the word <u>blassed</u>. It's irreverent to the blassed Vargin. Shay was a varry holy woman, and that's why shay's called blassed. The Bible says, 'All generations <u>shall</u> call mey blassed.' But yer don't care what the Bible says Yow thank that it doesn't matter a bat what Chrastians do, but yow'll just plyse yerself. Git last, yer nasty pag."

Mr Keymer had a missionary box with two slits in it arranged in the form of a Cross. "The long slat," he said was "toe put pannies through, and the short one for the saxpences." But one boy did not intend to contribute. "What are yow going to gave?" said Mr Keymer to him, holding out the box: "How much money have yer got?" "Sixpence, Sir." "Can't yer gave four pence of it? Yer don't want it, yer'll only waste it on swaytes, or other rubbish. Oh! Yer don't antand tow give anything; varry wall, I shall just reymember yow."

He had also some little green books for the children, marked one halfpenny: these he sold to them at a penny each.

Engaine in Essex, traditionally given to former headmasters of Christ's Hospital.

One a Monday morning there were generally some children whom he caned for misbehaviour in Church. "Yer dadn't know," said he, "that I was looking at yow; I saw yo through my railings."

I must not omit to mention Mr Keymer's amiable points. He had rewards for good behaviour. One of these was to have a plate of fine strawberries or cherries on the table of his study. After the lads had remained there about an hour, he said to them, "Now as today yow've bane varry good boys, I shall gav a strawberry to aych of the first two boys; only, the first boy must have the large one. If any of yow others want a strawberry, yo must try toe gat first tow. I won't kape yo any longer." The scholars then went out of the study in order, wistfully looking towards the plate. Another of his rewards was to invite his boys to come into his garden to weed it. On one occasion while they were weeding, he slipped a frog into the pocket of one of them. Then walking up to Jeffery, for that was the boy's name, "What's that yo've got in yer pocket?" said he. "Oh a frog! Yer don't ayte frogs, do yer?" Mrs Keymer lost a ring, which a boy who found it took to Mr Keymer's house. "Yo're a varry good boy," said Mr Keymer, "for finding thas rang" and, addressing, the servant, "Mary," said he, "Have yo a halfpenny?" Then continuing his words to the boy, "Now, I shall gav yow that halfpenny, for although yo gav mey a great dayle of trouble with yo're lassons, stall, as I said before, yo're a varry good boy for finding the rang."

On one side of Mr Keymer's garden was the Field of the C. H. children, a brick wall forming the division between the garden and the field. One the top of this wall Mr Keymer used to place an apple, and then remain concealed from view with a cane in his hand. Should one of the children in the Field happen to see the apple and try to get it, the master amused himself by defending it. I am sorry to say that some cruel boys had a spite against Mr Keymer's fowls, threw stones at them, and broke a leg of one of them.

Guy Fawkes day was a holiday, but of course everyone went to Church in the morning. The boys came to Mr Keymer's house to remind him of the horrible treason. He came out smiling and was quite prepared for the occasion. "Yo must all prass as close as yow can to the railing and have yo're hands ready" said he, "Because I want yer all to have a fair chance." Mr Keymer then beat their hands with prickly sticks which he had gathered out of his garden. Then he scrambled windfall apples, water and cinders. Some lads went away soaked with the water. The master was having a lark.

Chapter 9. THE SICK WARD

When a boy at Hertford was ill, or felt ill, he went to the Surgery of the Sick Ward to be examined by Dr Stone. If the doctor admitted him as an inmate, he was at once taken into the Sick Ward, and he had not even the responsibility of giving any notice to the Matron of his Ward which he had left. He remained at the Sick Ward till the day settled by the doctor for his exit. I was sometimes in the Sick Ward for a considerable time. What the ailments were which I suffered I do not know. Perhaps I never knew their names. And is it wonderful that a child should take no interest in such forbidding subjects as diseases? Besides, in this delightful place, pain was swallowed up by pleasure. The boys were very happy in the Sick Ward, and would have liked to live there always. There was delicious wholesome food, kind nurses, a warm comfortable room, a long table at which I read Dickens' "Pickwick Papers" and some good evangelical tracts. I liked the tracts, and thought that "Pickwick Papers" was a charmingly amusing book. The title page was missing, and I wondered who wrote it. When Dr Stone examined me after I had been for some days up and said that I was not strong enough to attend school yet and must remain in the Sick Ward for another week, the "woosent luxent" news filled me with such joy that I was afraid it would recover me too soon, and cause Dr Stone to change his mind. At this stage I had quinine every day at eleven o'clock, and I looked forward to the hour, for I was very fond of this tonic. Nowadays doctors are more shy of quinine than they used to be, having discovered that it may be bad for the heart.

There often came to see the patients a very kind and generous gentleman, whose name was Dr Lancaster. What kind of Doctor he was I cannot say; he was a wealthy man; he had no need to occupy himself in any work for the purpose of earning money, and I think he was free to use his time as he liked. It never fell to my lot to receive any gift from him, but I loved him for his kind words and the generous presents he made to others, who doubtless needed them more than I. I heard one of these sick boys say considerately to him: "I think, Dr Lancaster, the present you bring to us must be a great expense to you." The kind man replied, "Don't trouble about that, some persons are born with a silver spoon in their mouth, some with a gold. When I was born, there was a gold spoon in my mouth."

It was the opinion of Dr Stone that when a patient is alarmingly ill, it is right to give him any food he fancies. "There are three indigestible thing," said a medical man to me, "all of which begin with the letter P. They are pork, pickles and piecrust." "Why," I asked, "is piecrust inedible?" He replied, "I do not know." One of the children was so ill that his life was despaired of. "What shall

I give him to eat?" said the child's nurse to Dr Stone. "Ask him what he would like, and give him that," was the reply. He asked for pickles, and she gave him that.

Dr Stone once gave me a sudden sharp pain, but I had no doubt that he did so for my own good, and I was interested in his treatment. According to the instruction of my nurse, I lay on my back on the counterpane of my bed with my body bare and near the foot of the bed. I compared myself to a little balloon. Dr Stone, as he passed, gave the front of my body a sudden vigorous smack, and without any pause, continued to walk on to the door of the Ward, and went out.

The Sick Ward was a delicious relief to the scholars of Mr Keymer from their daily funk for him. But one day he made his appearance there. He came not for any pastoral purpose, but merely to persecute one of the patients. He said to him so that all the Ward could hear, "Yo'er shamming toe bay al. You've come here just beycause yer don't want too come to School. Vary wal. I shall raymember yow when yo come back again!"

Chapter 10. SUNDAY

On Sunday the children of Christ's Hospital, attended by their nurses, were taken to Hertford Church. Some of my Ward, No.8, liked to take hold of the hand of Mrs Meredith in starting for the country walk leading to it. On the way we heard the fine pealing of the Church bells, but I am sorry to say that, being hungry and miserable, I did not enjoy their music. The beautiful scenery of the Scotch mountains did not obtain appreciation from Dr Johnson, and probably because, in his time hotels were few and far apart and he could not get sufficient nourishment to give him the spirit to enjoy it.

Strange to say I remember most things of my childhood life but nothing of the Church, or its clergyman, or worshippers. It must have had a clergyman, because every Church of England Church has a clergyman. It probably had worshippers besides ourselves, and a steeple also, because on the last Sunday before the holidays we used to say:-

> "Goodbye Church, Goodbye steeple,
> Goodbye Priest and all his people."

Besides, I remember a conversation I had with a Christ's Hospital child who was a son of this clergyman. The boy was a little agnostic. He had the idea that nothing was certainly known of anything, and therefore there is no reason to be sure of the truth of anything. "You say," said he, "that God made the world, but we only know that from the Bible, and what if the Bible should not be true? Of course the world was created by some power or other, and that power you may, if you like, call God. I see no reason," he continued to say, "why it should not have been made by fairies or genii, but we cannot tell. We do not even know that we exist. The belief that we do may be a delusion. In dreams people think they see this and that, and at the time are convinced that the appearance is real, yet it turns out to be false. It may be, for aught you know, that your whole life is nothing more than a mere dream." It was crafty of Satan to tempt me by this child, who had, no doubt, got these ideas from grown-ups who were as spiritually blind as himself. What vexed me chiefly was that I could not give an answer which was satisfactory to myself to his suggestions. "What if the Bible should not be true?" I felt sure, as the Bible says itself, that every word of it is true, but at the early age of eight or nine I could not know anything of Paley's *Evidences*.[4] However I answered as well as I could. I said that the Bible is found to be true by all good Christian men. "These do not believe in fairies or genii, whom you think may have made the world, and even we children do not really believe in them, for we know that the stories about them are made up, and we

---
[4] William Paley, *A View of the Evidences of Christianity* (1794).

ourselves make up stories about them for our amusement." With my answer to his statement, "We do not even know that we exist", I was better pleased. I could not, at this early age, quote the famous argument of Descartes, "I think, therefore I am", to prove my existence, but it seems to me now that my answer implied this argument, for if I dream, although the persons whom I see in my dream do not exist, I must exist in order to dream. The following is what I said. I told him that it is one's duty to believe and act up to what he has no reason to doubt is religious truth even if he is in a dream. He must in his mind endeavour to do so. If life is a dream, one will at some point wake up from it. Then, the dream being over, it will be too late to do the duties of life, and he will be found guilty and punished for not having attempted them. If, on the other hand, life is found, at the end of it, to have been not a dream but a reality, he will be condemned and punished for shirking the faith and duties of religion, and the excuse, "I thought that life might be a dream and delusion" will prove to be of no use to him.

Perhaps some reader may ask, If truth has evidences, and men do not know what they are, are men at fault for hating and opposing truth, and for loving and choosing error? In reply I can say that Holy Scripture tells us that they indeed guilty, for they are disobeying the law that is written in their hearts, living lawless lives, like the beasts that perish; but Holy Scripture also informs us that although that is so indeed, they are, nevertheless, not so guilty as those persons who know what the evidences of truth are, and yet refuse to obey the truth. It gives us examples to illustrate this fact. The land of Sodom was not so guilty as Capernaum, and the soldiers who crucified Christ were not so bad as those of the Pharisees who fought against the truth when they knew it. We are told in the Bible that there are some sins that are greater than others, and we are also told there are some punishments that are greater than others.

One Sunday there was a heavy rain, and we could not go to Church, so we had the Prayer Book morning services in the Hall instead. Mr Ludlow, the Steward, read the service. In the middle of the Confession he shouted to a boy who was coughing, "Leave off barking, young monkey." This language of mixed metaphor amused me. "A monkey," I thought, "ought not to attend a religious service, because he has no sins to confess, and has no notion of its meaning. But how funny that a monkey should fancy that he is a dog and bark!" Much more appropriately Mr Ludlow afterwards read out of a book a sermon on the Rainbow which was suited to the state of the weather.

On the Evening of every Sunday Mr Keymer came into the Hall and read prayers and afterwards preached. The Girls of the Hertford Bluecoat's School also were present. The bell to announce service was rung for a considerable time although everyone was present except Mr Keymer. Between the prayers and sermons he left the Hall to change his surplice for a black gown and solemnly returned to the pulpit. The girls were from seven to eighteen years old, and sat in a row in such order that their heads formed a straight line verging to the ground. Those who were about seven were very interesting to me, and some were attractive, but those who were older were too big to please me. Burke in his "Essay on the Sublime and Beautiful" gives a philosophical reason for this. Smallness belongs to Beauty and Largeness to Sublimity. Given the same animal, the small is more endearing, the large more awe-inspiring. Thus, the girl who is pretty when she is small sometimes becomes too big to attract, and is then called a fine girl, just as the small cub of the lion and wins caresses, but when it is bigger it looks alarming. Jay of Bath took up the cub of a lion and fondled it, but would he have even touched it when it was older?[5] Smallness makes some atonement for the plainness of little girls, and causes ordinary defects of feature to be less forbidding. The age of the greater part of the girls was greater than that of any of the boys. I thought that some of the older girls were rather plain, one or two dubiously passable, and some even ugly. Perhaps the environment of a hard school-life was not favourable to the retention of good looks. It may have soured the disposition. It is probably true that till the age of 35 the faces of the fair daughters of Adam improve or grow worse according as they cultivate or neglect to cultivate an amiable disposition. However, Sunday evening was very pleasant to me on account of the presence of the little girls, one of them especially, and I rejoiced when they came into the Hall, and was sorry when they went out again.

Mr Keymer occasionally preached a funeral sermon. That was when a boy died. It was called "a jolly sermon" for it pleased the children to hear him speak kind words of the departed. I never heard the word "jolly" used at Christ's Hospital except on this occasion. "Jolly" was thought by the boys there to be the mild effeminate slang of school-girls, though strange to say, girls used the word much because they thought it was the slang of school-boys. I cannot recall anything of a funereal sermon of Mr Keymer, except the following words:-

"Hay was a varry good boy and always larnt has lassons wal, and af yo want toe go toe Havvn yo must bay like ham."

I can recollect one of the sermons of Mr Keymer. Although the girls were present, he was so rude as to speak of the flogging of boys with the birch rod. This I thought as indelicate as if he had spoken of the use of the birch by Miss P. and Miss L. for the punishment of the girls. The boys had great pity for the

---

[5] Rev. William Jay (1769–1853).

girls and believed that the greater part of them were almost angelical, and the rest of them far better than boys and too good to deserve this brutal treatment, though it was rumoured they frequently had it. At my early age I had never been acquainted with any girls except my sisters and they were apparently faultless. This was the sermon:-

"My day'r Chaldren, I shall take my text thas ayvenang from the Book of Common Prayer, or, as way often call at, The Prayer Book. The word 'Common' has a daffayrant maynang from what at used toe have. At now mains something that aynt worth much, but I have often told ye that the Prayer Book, like the Bible, is varry holy. Now my text as, 'That at may playse thay toe allumanayte all Bashops, Praysts and Daycons.' Yow all know what a clargyman as. Ganarally spayking, has is a varry good raylagious man, whose pleasure and duty as two taych raylagion toe others. That as the rayson payple always put 'Reverend' before has name. Yow must never forget toe ravarance a clargyman. My name as, The Ravarand Nathaniel Kaymer. Now there are some clargymen whom way should ravarance more than others, and that as the rayson way davide clargyman antoe thray orders – Bashops, Praysts and Daycons. Bashops are put first because way must ravarance them even more than Praysts; Daycons varry properly an the text are put last.

I was once a Daycon, but now I am a Prayst. But there are some payple an thas world who are so varry wacked that they don't ayvan thank of thayse dastanctions. Oh! They don't ravarance clargymen, they don't thank at worth the trouble. Now I warn yow, while yo're children, lest yow should grow wacked too. All of you promised an yo'er baptisms not toe bay wacked. Some of yo, I am afraid, often forget thas promise. Now the rayson way masters punish yow as only toe raymind yo. I daresay some of yo boys thank way are varry unkind when way punash yo; but at aynt so, no, not an the layst. Way only dow at from kindnass. Whan a boy tals may a lie, I always gave ham the barch-rod; but at asn't anny pleasure toe may toe do so. Quite the contrary. I always fale varry grayved. But af all the caning amd bayting way gav yo don't kape yo from growing wacked, than at's yo'er fault that yo can't go toe Havv'n. What does the Scripture say? 'The wacked shall bay turned antoe Hal'. 'Than shall hay say toe those on has laft hand, Daypart, yay cursed antoe avvarlasting fire praypared for the devil and his ayngals.'"

END OF CHRIST'S HOSPITAL, HERTFORD

At the age of 9 TRB was moved to the main site of Christ's Hospital in Newgate, London.

THE LONDON SCHOOL (1855-61)

LONDON WORDS

"Backs":	"I retract my agreement."
Bolio, A:	A bolster
A brushing:	A flogging with the birch rod
Brushing in public:	A flogging with a birch rod before the whole school
"Cuts for Hertford words"	Pinches for using Hertford words not used in London
"Cuts with the cane"	Strokes of the cane on the hand
Dab, A	An expert
"Fin":	"I forbid"
"Fin backs"	"I forbid you to say backs"
Fudge, to	To secretly prompt one who is saying a lesson
"I shall throw it away"	This is said to induce a coy person to accept an offered gift. "If you don't accept it, it will be wasted, for I shall throw it away"
Jicker	Salad dressing
Mag, to	To scold (Nag is not used)
Mouldy	Not appreciated, not liked
On the sly:	Secretly done
"Over to the left":	Negation to what is said. Thus I shall does such a thing over the left, means, "I shall not do it"
Pigging	Removal from one Ward to another
Prig, A	A thief (No other meaning at C.H.)
Prig, to	To steal, thieve. (The prig of novels was unknown at C.H.)
Scaf, A	One who does not give to an asker
Shark, To:	To ask for a little
Sharker, A	An asker. A sharker is not a voracious person, not like a shark. Illustration: - "The sharking money-box" – The box collecting money, asking for it
Snitch, A	A dull, uninteresting person

Spadge, to	To walk in a stately manner, moving so as to describe in space waves with pointed summits, each step describing a gulf between the highest point of a wave, and that of its successor
Stunning	The opposite of Mouldy. Very pleasant.
Swob, A	A servant. (Fag was not used in the sense of servant at Christ's Hospital)
Toughy, A	One who does not groan or utter a sound when put in pain by a bully.

Chapter 11. WARD NO. XV

The Wards of Christ's Hospital, London, were 16 in number containing about 50 boys in each Ward. There was also a Sick Ward. I was placed in Ward XV, the Nurse of which was Mrs Stag, and after the Pigging (Removal to another Ward) in Ward X. Of these two Wards alone I can write, having had no experience of the rest except the Sick Ward. The rooms of Nurse Stag, and the bed and study of the Grecian[1] of the Ward may first of all be mentioned. The Grecian's study was small and his bed was outside it. The bed had a curtain round it to make it private. The Grecian had a swob (servant), some lad of the Ward, whose social extraction no doubt was plebeian. The swob made the Grecian's bed, blacked his boots, and when called, obeyed his orders. The Grecian had a lofty manner like that of a giraffe, and was a grand being. He took no notice of anyone in the Ward except his swob. It seemed very wonderful to the boys of No. XV that the Grecian in his study had actually condescended to have a pleasant little chat with this servant, and moreover, the swob boasted, "He put some lavender-water upon my handkerchief."

Nurse Stag was able to be more sociable. She told us that she had visited Rome, and that in one of the Churches there the head of John the Baptist was shown to her and to other visitors. The exhibitor was doubtless a wag, for, when she made the objection, "I have already seen the Baptist's head in another Church and he cannot have had two heads!", she received the reply, "O yes, one of the heads belonged to him when he was a young man, and the other when he was older!"

Her sociability also was shown by the following. There was a lad who had a gift for public speaking. He delivered a mock sermon on the words, "They are coming!" which he said he took for his text, meaning that the French were coming to invade England. The Nurse came down from her rooms and listened to the sermon throughout. At that time the mind of the Christ's Hospital boys was much upon the Napoleonic wars. It was the absurd idea of these boys that one British soldier could chase a hundred Frenchmen. Another lad was a good entertainer. He sang "The Cork leg" with perfect action,[2] and he admirably imitated Mr Keymer, the Grammar School Master of Christ's Hospital,

---

[1] This is one school term TRB did not seem to think it necessary to translate - and indeed, it's in the *OED*: B.2.b "A boy in the highest class at Christ's Hospital (the Blue-coat School)."

[2] A comic song about a Dutch merchant whose cork leg continues to operate long after his own demise. Imagine, if you will, a steampunk hybrid of *The Red Shoes* and *The Terminator*.

CHRIST'S HOSPITAL, LONDON

Hertford.

It was one of the duties of the Nurse to be present with the lads when they washed. There was no objection to this, for they only washed the head and neck and feet, and she directed them to show the neck to her after it had been washed. "You hav'n't washed your neck," she said to one. "Yes, I have, Mum." "Go and wash it again, I could sow mustard and cress in it." He did not wash it again, but after a time showed it to her once more. Then she said, "It's beautiful now." The place in which the boys washed was a long room called "The Lavatory" containing a row of taps with a gutter underneath. The washing in the Lavatory was a pleasant affair. The boys, bared down to the waist, placed the neck and the head under the row of taps of running warm water, and they helped one another to dry the head, holding a towel tight and drawing it backwards and forwards over the head. The ground of the Lavatory was slimy, but that did not matter, for before drying a foot, they could hold it under a tap, and the slime was removed into the gutter.

Every boy had a face-flannel. It was not really wanted, for he could lather his hands and use them better. But one thing was important. If he took it from its numbered peg in the Ward cupboard, he had to be careful to take it back again. Otherwise he gave trouble to Mrs Stag , and committed what, in her theology, was a grievous sin. This Nurse, not knowing better, did a dangerous thing. She put a nail on to the end of a long stick reaching almost the length of the Ward to give a reminder to anyone at a distance who was not listening to her. It swayed up and came down with a force that she did not intend.

A great deal of the boys' time in the evening, sometimes all of it, was wasted by her "magging" of some lad before the whole Ward. M. asked if he might keep his Bible through the week, for the Bibles were being put away into the cupboard until next Sunday should come. "What do you want it for?" said the Nurse. "You'll only dirty it." Another boy, N., interferes, "Please mum, M. wants to be a clergyman." "The Nurse replies, "Don't you talk, N., M. is much more fit to be a clergyman than you are, M. is a good boy, and you are not." N. mutters for the boys near him to hear, "What have I done? I've done nothing; the old hag is magging at me for nothing at all." Nurse:- "I won't have you answering, N.; I didn't tell you to speak." N.:- "I was saying that I've done nothing." Nurse:- "None of your impertinence, N., mind that I don't report you to the Steward." One day, but it was earlier, she boxed the ear of a lad of a fiery disposition. I am sorry to say he at once gave her a violent blow in the face with his fist. She was surprised and asked him why he did that. "You hit me," said he, "and I hit you."

One of the Deputy Grecians - Monitors - Machin, was the most cruel bully I ever knew. It was his pleasure to send the other Monitor, Douglas, to the end of the Ward to listen while he dropped a pin on to the Monitors' table, and say whether or not he heard the sound. If anyone in the Ward made the faintest rustle or even audibly breathed, Machin called him out, put the head of his victim on to the Monitors' table, and brought down his fist on to that unfortunate's back with a mighty thump. On one occasion the heavy thuds of the cruel blows and the pitiful groaning brought out the Nurse from her sitting-room to complain. Machin in a violent passion told her that he kept order in the Ward for her benefit, and that, instead of being thanked, he was blamed, finishing his reproaches by swearing at her. She fondly thought now that he was in her power, and replied that she would report him to the Steward for swearing at her. Machin appealed to Douglas, "Did I swear?" "No," said Douglas. "But I plainly heard you," protested the Nurse. Machin and Douglas both took their oath that she was mistaken.

Machin was regarded in the Ward as a "Russian bully"; some thought that he was indeed a Russian. Recently (1853 and 1854) England had been at war with Russia, and the boys were told about the cruel Russian treatment of the Poles. I was but 9 or 10 years of age, and in the absolute power of this human brute, nearly double my age. He used to inflict horrible suffering upon me for his savage amusement because I was "a toughy" - one who could bear pain without groaning. He used to make me jump as high as I could, and when I was well above the ground, box my ear, driving me in the air. He asked me once if I, being a Christian, loved him, according to the commandment, "Love your enemies." I said nothing but was gratified to find that the knowledge in the Ward of my Christianity extended to the Monitors. A Christian does indeed love a bad man as a possible future convert, but not as a hater of God and his people. The other monitor Douglas neither befriended me nor did me harm.

The Deputy Grecians, like the Grecian, had a "swob". Some lad, not of gentle birth, would be willing to be the Monitors' swob. He made their beds, blacked their boots, made coffee and toast for them, and afterwards coffee and toast for himself. Machin and Douglas's swob showed that he was a "snob" (blackguard) by gobbing (spitting) over some toast and coffee, and then giving it to a lad who knew nothing about this defilement. The Monitor Douglas for his own amusement acted better. There was nothing "poling" (defiling) in slate-pencil dust, ink, sugar, salt, mustard and pepper. He made a dose of these ingredients in the presence of a lad who agreed to take it into his mouth for the reward of some hot coffee and buttered toast to follow it. I think there was also the additional reward of sixpence. The dose flew a long distance out of the lad's mouth on to a beautifully clean freshly sanded floor of the Ward. The Monitor was satisfied and gave the promised rewards, and the good meal immediately took away the vile taste of the dose.

This Monitor used to get from one end of the Ward to the other by silently running from one bed to another without touching the ground. One night when he touched Green's bed, which was next to mine, Green made a loud cry like that of a hyena. Douglas, startled, took a tremendous leap; Green said it was "over three beds", but it could not have been so much as that. Douglas, looking amused, came to Green and asked him, "What made you make that unearthly noise?" "I was dreaming," replied Green. After Douglas had gone away, Green said to me, "I was not asleep, I made that row for a lark."

Sunday was not disliked at Christ's Hospital, not even by irreligious boys. They were not forced to play the brutal games described elsewhere, and they were not so much bullied as on other days. When a library was provided, blue rag covers were placed on books selected from the others for Sunday reading; and some wholly secular books had these blue covers put on them by mistake. It did not matter, the blue covers turned the secular books into sacred ones. "That is not a Sunday book." "Oh yes, it is, it has a blue cover." These blue books had little or no Divinity in them. I preferred my own religious books purchased from outside, especially Bunyan's treatises, of which I read a great many. It was the function of the monitor D. to supervise a reading of the Bible in the Ward on Sunday afternoon. He sat on a chair and we on the settles at the end of the beds, and we read a verse in turn. On one occasion he fell asleep, and when we came to the end of the chapter, the last verse which had only six words was repeated by everyone in turn until the monitor awakened. "Have I been asleep?" said he. "Yes." "Why didn't someone awake me?" "We didn't like," replied one.

If the matron had chanced to come to the spot, he might have been reported to the Steward, and dismissed from office.

I tried to make some amends for the disadvantage of being without Sunday School teaching, and learnt by heart several passages of Scripture, and some of

Dr Watt's Divine Songs for children. Dr Johnson, being asked his opinion of this poetry for children, replied that it is not very good, but it has the merit of being better than anyone else's.

CHRIST'S HOSPITAL, LONDON

Chapter 12. THE WRITING SCHOOL

In the Writing School Mr Griggs, Mr Sharp and Mr Mackay taught us Writing and Arithmetic. Mr Fitzjohn and Mr Sykes, Spelling, Reading and Dictation, and the Royal Genealogy; and in another room Mr Bowker, Geography and English History.

Writing was very well taught. The masters were most particular as to the way we ought to hold our pens, and we had to be very careful to make the top end of the holder point to the right shoulder. It was thought that I should some day obtain "the gold pen" which was awarded once a year to the best writer. An elder brother, who was with me at Christ's Hospital, obtained it, but I was not successful. The value in money was said to be seven pounds. He had the honour on Speech Day of presenting a beautiful specimen of his penmanship to the Lord Mayor, and was generously rewarded by that dignitary with a gift of five sovereigns. In my days at school, rules for writing were better known in the world than they are now, better steel pens were made, and better paper. We had correct copies in the copybooks for our imitation, which I never see in the copybooks sold in the present day.

To speak of the Masters of the Writing school in turn, beginning at the lower classes, I think that the first master here who taught me was Mr Sykes, once a Master at Hertford, but now removed to London. Either he or Mr Fitzjohn gave the boys an impossible task. I wish I could remember which master of the two it was. The boys were told to copy down the Royal Genealogical Tree from William the Conqueror to Queen Victoria, with its Houses of York and Lancaster and the rest, from a printed card on to a school slate. Of course if writing were sufficiently reduced in size, the thing could be managed, for the whole of the Lord's Prayer has been inscribed on the top of the point of a needle, and I have seen it through a microscope. But ordinarily there is a reasonable limit to capacity. When an omnibus is full, it refuses to take twenty more passengers. Captain Stephens says that the llama will carry a hundred pounds weight, but neither blows nor coaxing will induce it to exceed that amount. I cannot solve the mystery of the master's requirement, and therefore shall pass it by without further comment.

Near Mr Sykes was Mr Mackey. He gave instruction in Arithmetic and Writing. He was said to be son-in-law to Mr Brooks, the Steward. Mr Mackey and all the teachers of Writing were careful to maintain a high standard of excellence in penmanship. If a boy looked pleased with himself, Mr Mackey said, "That would please your mother, but it will not do for me."

As to his manner of teaching Arithmetic, I recollect the following. He would say, "I know you like eating sugar-sticks better than doing lessons, so I'll try to teach you by talking about them. (Draws a vertical chalk line upon the blackboard.) There's a sugar-stick. You can fancy it's divided between you. Now turn your heads this way. How do you divide fractions? I told you last time you were here that the rule for the divisor is to turn it upside down and multiply. That's simple enough, but I suppose I must explain it again. If you had a glass of wine, what would you do with it? Can you answer that? (A boy) Turn it upside down. (Mr Mackey) Well! All I can say is you'd be very foolish. I should never waste a glass of wine like that. What! Turn a glass of wine upside down? Ha, ha, ha, he, he, he, I should take good care first to have my mouth underneath.

The next master was Mr Fitzjohn. He generally entered the School panting. He was a big man and of such a weight that his chair creaked under him. Have you ever, Reader, seen a dish brought to the dinner-table with only one enormous potato on it and a number of baby ones? "It would be too ridiculous," you say. But just as absurd appeared this stout man with his class of diminutive scholars. On his arrival at school in a gasping condition, he sank into his chair, and thoroughly wiped his face, ears and neck with a large red pocket handkerchief. One day after this cooling process was finished, he addressed the class in a tone of affection. With a mournful glance, he uttered a few tender words, scarcely audible, as if he thought they might be the last words he was about to speak on earth. "Dear boys, be very good and quiet today, for I am feeling ill. Don't give me any trouble: I am too weak to keep you in order. I ask of you a special favour this morning. Be so kind, dear boys, as not to make a noise. I can hardly speak." The last words were repeated in a just audible pianissimo. "I can hardly - speak."

We were sorry. These were kind expressions, and condescending also, and we felt that we must be very hushed and gentle. But one lad was a slight exception. He thought that he might, without harm, drop a pencil or say something. Then the unexpected happened. "You rascal," shouted the master in a tremendous voice probably louder than that of Stentor, whose words could be heard above the din and clang of battle. Mr Fitzjohn had recovered. "You rascal, come down here, and I'll thrash you soundly. Come down here, Sir: I'll teach you your duty. If you can't be persuaded by fair means, you shall by foul. I see that you intend to be master here." We were almost stunned with surprise and fear. Where was our pity now? It was transferred to the little chap he was so unmercifully dressing.

Opposite Mr Fitzjohn was Mr Sharp. Mr Sharp was an authority on the art of penmanship, and cut exquisite quill pens. He writing was very beautiful. In making ornamental flourishes of every kind he never made a miss, and he had perfect command of a ruler. I got on very well with Mr Sharp, and the other Masters of the Writing School, for I was fortunately a good writer. In arithmetic his method may be shown by the following dialogue.

(Mr Sharp to a boy.) "What is discount?" No answer. (Mr Sharp) "I must say, it is most incredible; I ask a plain question, and I can't get an answer." (Boy forced to reply) "Interest, Sir." (Mr Sharp, excitedly making a complete revolution of himself on one heel.) "Absurd in the extreme. Well! That beats me. The fellow must be a downright fool. I ask a plain question, and that is the answer I get. Did you intend to insult me, Sir? However, I suppose there must be some thorough blockheads in the world. I'll try another question, perhaps it's too difficult; have you got a head on your shoulders?" (Boy) "Yes, Sir." (Mr Sharp) "He actually knows it. I shouldn't have thought he would have known that. He's got a head! But it's a head with uncommonly little knowledge in it. I know what you think. That when you leave School, you're going to do nothing but walk about the streets like a fine gentleman, with your hands in your pockets. But I can tell you, young man, you're mistaken. You'll find out then, when it's too late, what a blockhead you are."

The last master in the room, and the head one in it, was Mr Griggs. He used to say at every writing lesson, "Between the thick and the thin, the width of an o, between two thicks, rather less than the width of an o, and <u>today</u>, boys, I want your very best writing." In arithmetic, Mr Griggs taught Tare and Tret, Stocks, and other commercial sums. I listened to his explanations in vain, for I did not understand his commercial terms. He made allowances for me on account of my good writing.

Downstairs was Mr Bowker. He had a classroom to himself, where he taught us Geography and English History. This gentleman had great literary knowledge and was a member, I believe, of learned societies.

Geography Mr Bowker did not teach well. He gave us maps to copy, and that was all. We took care to draw and paint our maps well, and to copy correctly a few principal names. One lad executed his work artistically; he spared no time and pains over the name of the country, and he even glazed his map with gum, so that it looked almost as if it had not been drawn by hand. The master could not help admiring the work, but remarked that it had not many names.

Some of us could not see to copy the small names in maps. Astigmatic sight was not then understood by oculists, and the only thing we could do was to invent names, and for our purpose, the Ward List of surnames of boys was most helpful. Once there was danger of being found out. "What is this?" said the master, "there is no such place," but something drew off his attention, and the matter ended.

When once Mr Bowker had lost the attention of his class, he had not always the power of keeping order. One lad and then another from different ends of the room would, for a lark, slam a desk, and the master chased backwards and forwards slashing his cane; and there soon was a general slamming and running about. I was very sorry for this foolery, and did not join in it. It was ill-mannered and ungrateful, for though Mr Bowker sometimes got in a wax, he was a gentleman well-disposed and pious.

I shall repeat here some of his instructions. "Boys, it isn't everyone who has had the privilege of travelling in foreign countries. Now you all know, because I have told you, that I have travelled a great deal. Some persons who travel get very conceited; others get experience and information, and are then able to instruct those who read or hear what they have to tell. I have travelled about Switzerland, and have been on some of its high mountains, and have seen so many places that it would take me too much time to name them all; so I have the advantage of knowing the truth of what is reported by travellers. Some of those fellows tell the biggest lies a scoundrel can invent. There's that Arthur ____. You must not believe a word that fellow says. But I can tell you at the same time that I have heard and seen many wonderful things which you would scarcely believe, and which nevertheless you know to be true because they are told to you by me. There's a field of corn in Australia of which I will tell you the history. Once, a long time ago, a gentleman was showing me a mummy. The mummy held in his hand some of that ancient Egyptian corn which grew 2,000 years ago. Fancy! This corn had been held 2,000 years in the hand of the mummy! Well, I begged a little of this corn, and the gentleman kindly gave me a few grains. These I sowed in my garden. They produced a crop, and that crop a larger one, and so on until at last there was this large field of corn in Australia. All that came from the few grains given me from the mummy's hand.

"There is another story I can tell you of a mummy. It was the body of Henry the 7th. I am told that only a few years ago his coffin was opened, and there he lay with the same avaricious look that he had when he was buried, for the features were perfectly preserved by an airtight metal coffin. Indeed, there were three coffins, the second one encasing the first in which the King lay, and the third encasing the second. It is now time to serve out the history books. We have today to read about Titus Oates. Ah! he was a knave. He was worse than Marlborough. A most thorough knave that fellow was. Marlborough was avaricious, but he had some good qualities, and he was an able general. Marlborough too was very deceitful. But Titus Oates was not only avaricious and deceitful, he was bloodthirsty. Titus Oates was the greatest scoundrel that ever walked this earth. This infamous scamp had terrible sufferings, but he richly deserved his punishment. The Bible says, 'Bloodthirsty and deceitful men shall not live out half their days.'"

These things were interesting and deserved attention and gratitude, and for a time they had it. But, perhaps, Mr Bowker was too long. Most persons, grown-ups as well as young, cannot listen for more than few moments to instructions. Only a few can with pleasure exert themselves to give to a grave and learned man the attention that is due to him. So it happened that a lad, born perhaps like the majority with sluggish brains, was suddenly seen by the master to be woolgathering. Mr Bowker was at once irritated, and when one is irritated, the mind becomes like a distorting looking-glass that takes an ugly view of anything in front of it. In his excited state he called this boy the very name which he had been applying justly to Titus Oates. "See that Knave!" Mr Bowker cried. "I may talk, and talk, and talk, and talk, and the fellow doesn't listen to one word I'm saying. Come out here, you scoundrel, you scamp, you infamous rascal, and I'll give you a baker's round dozen."

Chapter 13. GAMES

There were two rough and cruel games which could only be enjoyed by the biggest boys, but everyone in No. 15 Ward was obliged to attend, and the boys' names were called out from the Board belonging to the Ward by one of the Monitors. These games were "Hunting the Stag" and "Storming the Castle". The "stag" was represented by some strong lad, say "the buck of the ward" who would, during the game, punch with his fists anyone who came near him. When the stag was at length overpowered and seized, he was carried by several big lads to the goal, some holding his arms and some his legs. The cruel part of the affair was that a little boy was placed under the back of the stag to support it, and this little boy who was necessarily bent down under the weight, was hurried along faster than his legs could conveniently carry him. He was in the dark too, for the stag was surrounded by a running crowd of lads, and he sometimes was exhausted and trampled upon. When the little boy thus became a failure, another little one was forced to take his place.

In the game "Storming the Castle" the lads of the Ward were divided into two opposing armies. They faced each other under an archway. The duty of one of the armies was to prevent the other from pressing its way through the archway. The cruelty in this game was that the big lads in the attacking party clambered over the heads of the little ones. The games of cricket and football were not, to my knowledge, ever played in the London School for there was not field or suitable place for them. The favourite game was Rounders. I did indeed once see a football kicked by a Grecian in the playground adjoining the Hall, but he only spadged after it, and called to some lad, "Here, fetch me that ball," while as he spadged, the skirts of his coat flopped about his legs. I never saw a Grecian run, or with his skirt tucked up into his girdle. Such a thing would have been "*infra dig*" in the presence of others. What Grecians did behind our backs I cannot say. I don't remember any other games of the London School, except "Puss in the Corner" played by little boys in that cloister which was denoted by a text upon it, "Honour all men, &c." (1 Peter II.17)

There was not much inclination for play in the London School. The scholars could neither skip so well, nor play at marbles so well as when they were at Hertford, for they had lost much of their former ability from want of practice. Skipping was felt to be girlish, and playing at marbles, childish. They wasted hours looking through the bars of the School at the people passing, and wishing themselves outside. There were a few absurd amusements which ought to be mentioned because they had the merit of lessening the dreariness of this prison life. One of them was to observe by the clock how long one could stand on a slanting ledge which lay at the bottom of the "Garden" wall. A lad got so expert that he stood reading a book for half an hour when, forgetting that his feet were on the slant, he paced forward and nearly fell. Another amusement requiring much time and perseverance was making horsehair chains ornamented with beads, and making cherry-stone chains, which latter were very trying to the patience, for after grinding each link, it had to be cut and there were many failures. With such recreations, these cloistered scholars were indeed much more like monks than boys.

CHRIST'S HOSPITAL, LONDON

Chapter 14. THE HALL

A cloth cap is part of the dress of a Bluecoat boy. To establish this fact a formality was performed at certain set times. The whole School, ever scholar wearing a cap, was paraded through the cloisters, and inspected by the Steward before the Hall door. The cap was not made to fit, it was stiff and flat like a biscuit, but it could be carried on a steady head for about ten minutes, the required time, and if it fell it could be picked up and balanced again.

The Hall was a fine building. To give a full description of its merits would require a good knowledge of architecture. It possessed some grand old paintings. One of them in the Organ-loft represented an encounter of a man with a shark. The Organ was a magnificent instrument. It was played in a masterly style by the celebrated organist Mr Cooper. He conducted the singing of the School. I remember that he made the words "And make them fall" in the National Anthem, very staccato. Also I recollect two lines of the air and words of an Anthem, the words composed by a Grecian, and the music by Mr Cooper.

Key G.

    d | f : m | m : r | t d l t | d :-

The feathered   songsters tune their throats

Ta | l : f m | r : s | t l | l : s ||[3]
To greet their new-ly risen king

Mr Cooper, although a first rate musician, was not popular with the boys. He encroached too much on their play-time. They, therefore, sometimes refused to sing, or else sang wrong words. Then descending from the loft, he held a consultation with Mr Brooks, the Steward. After the threat from the Steward, "Boys, your Leave Day is in jeopardy" and one or two more ascents and descents, Mr Cooper gave up the attempt to conquer, and the School lost its monthly outing for the day. In Christ's Hospital, however well-behaved a boy might be, he was liable to punishment. I shall leave the Reader to decide as to its justice. For example, an individual in a Ward called out something rebellious and no one in the Ward would betray him, for no one could do that with honour.

---
[3] TRB was a great advocate of the Tonic Sol-fa system, the notation of which he is using here.

To meet the case the Steward gave two cuts of the cane to everyone in the boy's Ward. He did not punish the whole Ward for its refusal to inform but to make sure that the transgressor had been dealt with.

The meals in the Hall were preceded by Duty. That was a service of psalm-singing followed by prayers read by a Grecian. The Grecians entered, each one by himself, after all the boys were seated. All eyes were fixed on them as they passed from one end of the Hall to their dining-table at the other end. The boys noticed their style of spadge, how their girdle buckle hung, the colour of their kid-gloves, the whiteness of their bands, how their handkerchief showed from the pocket, and so forth. One Grecian would have a monocle held by the eye, another the same article dangling by a string. I looked with admiration upon a certain Grecian who refrained from following the foolish fashion of his fellows by a studious effort to avoid any appearance of spadging. Now it must not be supposed from the above description that the Grecians were merely young swells. No, they were the most advanced scholars Christ's Hospital possessed. They remained longer in the School than the rest, and had a good classical and mathematical knowledge.

My friend Jeffery for his amusement composed a bogus parliamentary speech about the Corn Laws, and placed it, before the time the Grecians entered, in their path. One of them, supposing that another Grecian had dropped it, picked it up. This was exactly what Jeffery intended, and he was gratified to see all the Grecians having a good laugh over it. It was full of spicy words, an unintelligible jargon, and they tried in vain to find who was the author of it.

An account of our dinner would not be very interesting. In a few words I shall say that on Saturday we always had soup, which was never eaten. It was called "mess". On Tuesday we had pork. This was preferred to the meat of other days. I praise the Christ's Hospital authorities much for providing that the bones that contained marrow should be cracked for the boys, and also that there were plenty of marrow-scoopers at hand for their use. The marrow was spread by us on bread and considered a great delicacy.

One day in the year we had pease pudding and pork. I think the meal was provided by a benefactor. On the occasion the scholars had a double allowance of food. But pease pudding is so nourishing that one could not eat much of it conveniently, and therefore half the amount went back to the kitchen. In summer time salad was provided, the dressing of which was called "jicker."

The bladebone was never eaten, for if one ate it he could be "poled" by it (made unclean) and be "put into coventry" by the boys. If meat were high, one could tell the Steward, but, as at Hertford, I never knew him to admit the fact. He would take a morsel into his mouth, spit it out again onto the clean and sanded floor, and pronounce it "very good".

The most interesting affair in the Hall was Supper in Public. The following rhymes about it were known by the scholars. Who was the author? I do not know.

> "Gentlemen and ladies, walk up the stairs,
> See the hungry lions and the half-starved bears,
> The stiff-necked pelican and the over-grown ox,
> The squeaking hurdy-gurdy and the sharking money box."

The "lions" were the Grecians, the "bears" the rest of the School: the "pelican was the "Treasurer", the "ox" the Steward, the hurdy-gurdy, the Hall's magnificent organ, and "the sharking money box" the box asking money for the Grecians leaving for College.

On a Supper-in-public we ate, in addition to the ordinary meal, "cruggy nailers", that is Captain's biscuits, which were hard, but pleasant to the taste.

At one Supper-in-public I saw the Duke of Wellington, the Waterloo celebrity. As he passed us, he patted the cheeks of one of the lads of our Ward, No. X. Was not that lad honoured to be thus noticed by this great benefactor of the British nation? The Duke of Wellington is one of three worthies that I am glad to have seen. The other two I saw outside Christ's Hospital, Queen Victoria, also a benefactor of our beloved country, by her bright example of righteousness to her subjects, and Dr. Zamenhof, a very modest man, but a benefactor of the whole world by his marvellous invention of the International Language.[4]

Chapter 15. THE DRAWING, FRENCH AND MATHEMATICAL SCHOOLS

Let us now go in thought to the Drawing School. Mr Back was the Master there. He taught drawing well, but some of his scholars did not make fair progress in return for his pains. When he looked at a performance of any one of these, he lamented in a loud weeping tone as he cuffed them vigorously, "When will you learn, you fool? Look at the model, you fool." Next to me sat a Scotch boy, Mackenzie, who could draw a little better than these dull ones but always failed in his attempt to form a good circle. His figure was like a damaged hoop. On one occasion, eyeing my circle with envy, he dug his pencil across it. Sometimes out of school time he used to draw for his amusement. In shading his picture he would make one part too dark. To correct this he made the lighter part too dark, so that the darker part was now not dark enough, and he put on it another layer of black. This he corrected by putting too much black on the light part, and the whole picture had the appearance of a large blot. Now although Mackenzie had a very good opinion of himself, he admitted to me that he must have made some mistake. He threw his performance into the fire and said "I will try again". But being too proud to listen to any explanation or suggestion he converted a second picture into another large blot.

I enjoyed Mr Back's instruction; it has been most useful to me ever since I was with him. One day when with others I was in the Latin School in Mr White's study, Mr Back came to see him. After prefatory cordial greetings, Mr Back said, "The object of my visit is to ask you to kindly give a name, perhaps a Latin name, to a small stick used to measure a drawing-model." Mr White, looking at it, replied, "It already has a name, it is a skewer." The drawing master admitted, "It certainly does look like a skewer, although it is not used as one." "But surely," replied the Latin master, "we cannot correctly say that a skewer is like a skewer." Mr Back was too polite to contend the point, and as he had come to Mr White for a name, he thanked him, and said that he would call the measuring stick by the name skewer. Henceforth in the Drawing School one heard these weeping lamentations over cuffed dull scholars, "Put the skewer to the model, you fool." "That's not the way to hold your skewer." "When will you learn how to use your skewer?"

---

[4] Ludwig Zamenhof (1859-1917). TRB became an Esperantist in 1906, one year after his son Christie.

CHRIST'S HOSPITAL, LONDON

The only modern foreign language taught at Christ's Hospital was French. For the study of this there was a French School, which had a Head Master, Mr Delittle, and second master, Mr Geney, both Frenchmen. The latter was my instructor. In remember a scene in which Mr Delittle took part. One day, before his arrival at School, a lad of his class was kicking about a large book just as if it were a football. Suddenly before the offender was aware Mr Delittle entered the room, and exclaimed, "I have caught you in the act. That is the way you treat the school-books in my absence!" "It was an accident, Sir, the book fell out of my hands as I was carrying it." "An accident! Why! I saw you raise your foot and kick the book." "No," replied the lad, "I take my oath that I raised my foot only to stop the book from falling to the ground after it had got out of my hands. I swear that it was an accident." This was indeed a shocking lie, but Mr Delittle said no more, probably feeling that the oath had put the matter out of his control.

There was nothing in this master's manner, accent or appearance to indicate that he was a Frenchman. It was otherwise with Mr Geney. He appeared to know English very imperfectly, and not to understand English boys, and he spoke and gesticulated like a foreigner. How it amused the class to watch his movements as he giggled over a book which he read to himself! They looked up with an enquiring smile. He told them that he was enjoying a play by Moliere, "The Miser", and he read aloud the passage that made him laugh where the principal character, the Miser, gets muddled in his repetition of a proverb, and renders it, "One must live to eat, and not eat to live." Then Mr Geney giggled again. The boys could not help laughing at the Master, and some of them, I am sorry to say, were so impolite as to imitate his giggles. But strange as it may seem their hilarity was quite misunderstood by the Master. He thought they were laughing at the joke, and so, in sympathy, he giggled still more. Soon the school was in a state of uproarious laugher, and Mr Geney ceased to be amused, and got waxy instead.

In the Mathematical School Dr Webster was the Head Master. I was not taught by him, but by Mr Gurney. Mr Gurney was a pious and just man. I much enjoyed his instruction in Euclid and Algebra, and got safely over <u>Pons Asinorum</u>. A lad, commencing Euclid with me, said that he did not like it. I asked, "Have you made any effort to learn it?" "No, I haven't." "Perhaps that is the reason you don't like it. Make an effort to learn the Proposition for this morning." After School he said to me, "You were right, I took your advice, and I said my proposition perfectly, and I got a pass to go out for this afternoon. I shall like Euclid now." We were both much pleased. The master was exceedingly particular that we should not say "therefore" instead of "wherefore" and vice versa. When we erred, he lifted the fingers of his right hand, and brought them down, like the toes of a crab, so as to clutch the crown of our head with an emphatic "wherefore" or a "therefore". This kind of correction was painful to the nervous system as well as to the head. Another of Mr Gurney's habits I did not like, but it was less painful. Astigmatic sight was not then understood, and no glasses were provided for it. It was necessary to give the eyes a momentary rest from the book in order to see at all. But the glance upward was mistaken by the Master for inattention or want of concentration, and he said, "Keep your eyes on the book." One cannot blame him for a mistake which arose from universal ignorance; it was unfortunate.

Now I do not say that every member of the class was diligent and attentive, or that those who were, were always so. For sometimes the atmosphere had a somniferous effect on the whole class, and three hours seemed too long for hard thought. But one Tuesday afternoon, it was a puzzle to Mr Gurney that no one even at the commencement of study was so bright as he ought to be. Why was this? A lad suggested to him that Tuesday was the day that Christ's Hospital had pork for dinner, and that pork muddles the brains. Mr Gurney wittily replied, "Pork takes three hours to digest, so then at the time for leaving school you will be ready to commence your work here." This was not intended to be taken seriously, for he could not allow them to leave meanwhile.

One day when we were learning algebra a member of the class had a boldness to say to him, "Please, Sir, your hair wants brushing." To our surprise Mr Gurney said nothing, but immediately walked out of the School, and after a while, returned with the fault rectified. I admired him for this way of responding to the lad.

Mr Gurney was a good preacher. In those days there were two kinds of clergymen – those who did not say the LORD'S prayer in the pulpit before the sermon, and those who did. I could always tell, before a sermon commenced, whether it would be good or poor, by the difference, for I reasoned thus: "If a man is so deficient in intellect as to say again the same prayer that has already been said several times in the service, he cannot have the mental capacity to preach very well." Mr Gurney on one occasion came into the pulpit of our Christ's Hospital Church, Newgate Street. I had never heard him preach and I was glad to know that his sermon was going to be good as he did not say the LORD'S prayer in the pulpit He interested the boys, and as he was a pious man, his sermon was calculated to do them spiritual good.

I have nothing more to say about this excellent man, excepting that in the holidays I once saw him at the seaside minding his children's clothes while they were bathing. He held ropes which were attached to their arms to keep them from going out of their depth. As it happened, they were afraid to venture further than about the depth of their ankles into the water, but it was prudent of him to make sure of their safety.

Chapter 16: MORALITY OF C. H. BOYS

The morality of the Christ's Hospital boys compared favourably with that of another school to which two of my brothers went and with that of a school to which I went when I quitted Christ's Hospital. There was, I confess, a great deal of bad language used at Christ's Hospital, and I underwent a little persecution for being religious, but not very long. I was quite willing to bear it for Christ's sake. On one occasion I took note from the clock of the length of time I was bullied by a crowd of lads in their efforts to make me swear. They would have been satisfied, they said, if I would repeat only one bad word. I found that the period was three quarters of an hour. They punched me, and finally gave me a mock crucifixion in the playground, strapping me up above the ground to some railings. As these efforts were in vain, my Ward, No. XV, got to respect me, and I gained an influence. Even wicked lads would appeal to me for my opinion as to the depravity of those with whom they quarrelled, and I had to be very careful what I said. One of the swearing lads suddenly announced that he was going to lead a new life, and he gave tracts to the boys of the Ward, a thing I had never felt it my duty to do. After a few days of ridicule from his swearing friends, he returned to his old life, and was heard swearing with them again.

Stealing was held in abomination and indeed was very uncommon. If a thief were discovered, their unwritten law against talebearing was broken and they reported him to the Steward, put him in Coventry, or called to him "You are a prig." A prig meant a thief. The word was used only in that sense in Christ's Hospital, it never had the meaning given to it in novels. Snob also meant cad or low-bred person, and nothing else. Even bullies did not steal. There was a lad in one of the Wards who was suspected by certain lads of prigging. They treacherously united in a plot to tempt him to prig cake from a settle, in the night when the fellows were the asleep. One of the plotters was employed to beguile and instruct him. Their trap was successful. The poor prig was caught in the act. Next morning the plotters went in a troop to the Steward, and informed against him. Mr Brooks, after enquiry, told them that they were as bad as the thief, and declined to punish him.

CHRIST'S HOSPITAL, LONDON

It was a perfectly honourable thing with the boys to shark (ask). There was nothing in common between the voracious animal, the shark, and the sharker. The sharker was, like a missionary collector, contented with what could be spared, however small, and admitted the right to refuse to give anything. The refused sharker merely said, "You are a scaf." (One who does not give to the asker.) "When I have a parcel," said the refused one, "you will shark of me, and I shall give you nothing." This answer seemed reasonable. As if he said, "You have a perfect right to be a scaf to me, but when my turn comes I have the same right to be a scaf to you." Thus the ownership of property was fully recognized. If the reader wants any more light on the subject, the following proverb of the boys of Christ's Hospital may help to give it. "He that asks shan't have, but he that doesn't ask doesn't want." It was not prudent to be a scaf, but on the other hand, there were too many hungry lads sharking for small pieces. A lad with a cake once proclaimed in the Ward, "I am going to see whether you will allow me to have anything myself. I shall give to everyone who asks." At last he said, "I have now only this one mouthful left." A lad replied, "Give us a piece." (Why us instead of me, I do not know.) The poor cakegiver now said, "You have left me nothing at all!" Occasionally, therefore, it was wise to "tuck on the sly" - to wait till everyone in bed was asleep, and then take it from under one's bolio (bolster) and eat it in bed. There might be some lad after all not asleep. It would be prudent to give to him, and to do so with a good grace. Another plan was to go to "Sly Corner", a little beyond "Giff's Cloister", previously hiring one or two lads to watch at convenient distances and signal an approach. When a signal was heard, he who tucked on the sly pocketed his grub, and walked out slowly and unconcernedly before the visitor arrived. When the latter had gone, a return could be made to Sly Corner to finish eating the grub.

Friendship was frequently made by daily contact, and especially by sleeping next to another. Leggate I knew at Hertford. At London he was also with me in Ward No. XV. My bed for a time was by the side of his. As we lay in bed, we read the book of Job by the help of a light at our end of the Ward - each of us a chapter aloud alternately, but in a subdued voice. When a monitor or matron was near, we were silent.

When I went to another bed I slept next to Green. We saved up our pence, and called to the nurse's servant-girl as she passed our beds on an errand to buy her mistress's beer, and the rest, "Please buy us a Coburg loaf and half a pound of cheese." She was very obliging, and when the loaf came Green threw it up two or three times to the ceiling and we had a delightful meal on towny food. A new loaf from outside the School we liked much better than any cake or other sweet food, but usually were not able to purchase it except in the above way.

It was not possible to say one's private evening prayers except in bed, for the same monitor whose function it was to give the word of command, "Kneel", when all instantly fell on their knees, thrashed the unfortunate boy who was last in bed. If one was in danger of being last, it was prudent to get into bed as one was, and finish undressing under the bed clothes. Sometimes it was dubious as to who was last, and then there was no thrashing. Once I heard a monitor say to a big last lad, who was useful to him, "I can't spare you, I must treat you as I do all the rest."

There was no water in the Ward fit to drink. What there was, stagnant rain-water, I was sometimes obliged to drink to ease my suffering. The poor food put my digestive organs out of order, producing what we called water-brash. In the day-time I was better off, for my kind friend the Pump supplied me with a wholesome tonic. After every meal I vomited a white pulp, and then drank plenty of water. Finally I had gastric fever and was doctored at home for a long time. After the holidays, for the first week, I abstained from housey food. I ate every day three halfpenny Abernethy biscuits, one for a meal accompanied by plenty of pump water, and as we all had, after coming from home, something to eat, which was in our school-boxes, we were able to help one another.

CHRIST'S HOSPITAL, LONDON

Chapter 17. THE PLAYGROUNDS

There were several Playgrounds, one of which was called "the Ditch" and another "the Garden", but the Ditch was not a ditch, and the Garden was not a garden. In "the Garden" the nearest approach to a plant was our good friend in need, The Pump. It never allowed us to be thirsty, but we were often hungry and then it gave us water in plenty to make up for our want of food. One day, as hungry as a pack of wolves roaming over tracts of snow, the lads playing in the Garden saw trays of good things carried from the School Kitchen through the playgrounds to the Committee Room, where the Governors and Masters were about to dine. Mr Mackey, coming into the Garden some time before the hour for the dinner to commence, made some solemn remarks to the boys. Stopping the bearers of the trays to see what was under the lids, standing on tip toes, and raising every cover in turn, this master of the Writing School said, "Excuse me, boys, for not continuing what I was saying - Ah! cherry-pie! Very good! Ah! roast fowl! good! good! and that's roast beef! and that's baked potatoes!"

The bearers stood still while he did this. "Now boys," said Mr Mackey, "to return to what I was saying. I am now, as you see, wearing my hat, but before I mention the name of my Maker, I shall take it off. I am very particular to take off my hat before I am going to say the Divine Name. I do not want to take it in vain. I shall now take off my hat. Why do I do so? (A boy tells him.) What commandment am I now keeping? (No one cared to answer.) I am keeping the 3rd commandment. I refer to <u>God</u> who made you and me and all mankind. Now I may put my hat on again." Proceeding in his address, he again announced that he was going to take off his hat, and after that without any announcement he called attention to the action by a theatrical wave to the length of his outstretched arm. The boys could not imitate him now but they would be able to do so as soon as they left Christ's Hospital in towny clothes.

Out of school hours Mr Mackey superintended the library which was at one side of the Garden. It was a warm, comfortable room, made in my time. A deputy Grecian once spadged in, and having his ear boxed by Mr Mackey for omitting a salutation began to spadge out, but was detained in disgrace, and made to stand at a post.

In this playground there was a shop of which Mr Fletcher was the salesman. Packets of cocoa were bought here, also High pies and Low pies, and brandy snaps called jumbles. The cocoa was mixed with an equal amount of sugar and eaten in the solid state. High pies had a stiff crust, and contained cranberries, and, in their normal condition, plenty of juice. In appearance they looked like pork pies, and they had a hole in the top in the crust. Low pies were half an apple covered by a thin coating of sweet baked paste in a little saucer of well-sugared crust. The High and the Low were equally good, and each cost a penny, but I preferred to buy the Low for a very good reason. There were rascally-minded boys who would send a little lad for six High pies, suck out the juice from the holes at the top, and then return the High pies to be exchanged for low with the message to Mr Fletcher that the little lad or he had made a mistake. They had sent, they said, for Low pies. This happened so often that it could not be told whether or not the High pies were shams. Mr Fletcher was a well-meaning man but he had no means of knowing whether or not complainers were imposters, and therefore he suffered them to bear injustice.

Facing the shop, and in the middle of "the Garden" was the Pump. He who pumped had to be careful, for otherwise he would get a nasty knock from the handle when he took his hands off it. The first knock was instruction: any after knock was punishment for forgetfulness. Dear old pump, your water was excellent, the best food that Christ's Hospital supplied. There were two ways of drinking water, and by the choice of them the drinker showed whether he was a gentleman or a snob. The gentlemanly way is that approved in the Bible, making a bowl of the hands fitted together, filling it, and then drinking from that. It is said that Gideon's chosen men lapped like a dog, for the arms moving backward and forward acted like the tongue of a dog. The other method was the lazy way of putting one's mouth to the water. Thus some lads did not drink from their hands, but put their mouth to the spout of the pump, or very near it.

Now we are in the playgrounds I may mention that lads of one ward had as a rule little or no acquaintance with those of another ward. I knew a lad, Green, before the pigging from Ward XV to Ward X took place; we were together in both. He was much bigger than I, and as a true friend he thought that it was his duty to correct my faults by "cuts", pinches in the arm, but if I reproached him it was only by word of mouth. And once, when I imitated a grimace he made, he gave me a heavy box on the ear, and said, "That is to teach you not to play the fool." His theology was poor, for he told me that the best preparation one can make for heaven was to have a large family, thus obeying the command "Be fruitful and multiply". "The man who brings up a large family," said he, "lives an unselfish life." After a time Green became a Monitor of No.10, but the elevation made no difference to our friendship. One day in the playground called The Garden he said to me, "Poor little fellow. You're half starving, and I'm going to feed you." "Over the left?" I replied. Then in a grieved tone he said, "You know me better that that. I'm not a mean brute." He then gave me a huge hunk of cake. "Not so much," I protested, "you will not leave enough for yourself." "Then," said Green, "I shall throw the whole of it away, it's my duty to feed the hungry. What you don't eat you will be wasting. Eat and enjoy, and say no more." I was indeed hungry and managed to eat the whole hunk with comfort and had enough. "Poor fellow," he said, "it has made me very happy to be able to do you good."

Another lad, Sanders, whom I knew at Hertford and throughout my Christ's Hospital life, was an atheist. I tried to convert him, but was unsuccessful. The fellows were afraid to bully him, because he spent much of his spare time in fishing out knowledge of their secret faults. When they were about to molest him, he threatened to publish what he knew about them. He received an occasional blow, but did not return it, and he was fond of boasting to me about his morality, comparing it with the badness of others in the Ward. He watched between the arches of the cloisters to see where lads had their "fobs". "Fobs" were treasures hidden in the ground. He did not disturb these fobs but was contented with the satisfaction of knowing where they were.

In the playgrounds we saw Antony, the Beadle, marching by, or guarding some port or entrance. The boys remarked that he was fond of using spicy words. Probably he was only quoting Shakespeare or some other author. They used to tease him by reciting a rhyme about his nose. It was this:-

>   Antony's nose is long,
>   Antony's nose is strong,
>   'Twould be no disgrace
>   To Antony's face
>   If half his nose were gone.

He got angry or pretended to be.

Every now and then Mr Keymer came from Hertford to London on matters of business. Then his old scholars, meeting him in some playground, asked him questions. One lad, who had no brother at Hertford, said to him, "How is my brother at Hertford?" Mr Keymer replied, "Your brother as verry wal. Hay's a varry good boy: hay's first an the class; hay'll come toe London next time; I'm sure hay wal."

CHRIST'S HOSPITAL, LONDON

Chapter 18. THE GRAMMAR AND LATIN SCHOOLS

The first master I remember being under in the Grammar School was Mr Gaul. I recollect very little about him. In translating Caesar, when we came to the footman, he used to tell us that it did not mean "men that have kicking matches". I supposed he had a dislike to the game of football. His successor, Mr South, was a specimen of the rare old-woman variety of the human male. He spent much of the time of the school in magging one member of the class in the presence of the rest. Magging was a Christ's Hospital word for to scold like an old dame. For example the burden of one silly mag was that he would keep on writing letters to a lad's mother about her son's idleness until there was an amendment. This was not interesting to the rest of the class who heard quite enough of Mrs Candle-talk from the Nurses in the Wards. Another master in the Grammar School was Mr White. When Dr Jacobs, who, I believe, was not an Old Blue, became Head Master of the Grammar School, a new School, the Latin School, was formed for Mr White in Christ's Hospital, for it was felt that Mr White ought not to be under Dr Jacobs. Some of the Masters of the various Schools were Ward-visiting Managers. Mr White made it a crime to play at chess (why, I do not know) and threatened the birch for disobedience. Mr Bowker, his successor as Manager of Ward XV, turned the crime into a virtue, and gave the Ward several chess-boards.

After a time there was a general pigging, that is, removal from one Ward to another. Big lads were placed in separate Wards by themselves. The result of this pigging was that the bullying of little boys by big ceased. "Isn't it like heaven now?" said a little lad to me. "Not so good as that," I replied, "but much better than it was," for I could not agree that the change was like a removal from Hell to Heaven. But suddenly it occurred to me that perhaps the lad was speaking hyperbolically, so I added, "You are right, in a way."

Another good thing in the pigging was the appointment of Latin School monitors for the Latin School wards. The monitors of the Latin School wards were not so stuck-up as the Deputy Grecians, and did not consider it infra dig to speak in a friendly way to the lads they governed.

On entering the Latin School I was taught by Mr Wingfield. I remember nothing about him excepting that he used the cane a good deal. Then Mr White became my master, a venerable-looking old man with a strong likeness to Alexander Cruden,[5] the author of a concordance to the Bible and Apocrypha. Mr White wore spectacles, and had long white hair waving over his shoulders. When he called us into his study, he was supposed to be hearing our lessons, but we were usually doing nothing for most or all of the time, sometimes a whole hour. A lad was placed in front of us with a slate to take down the names of any who made the slightest sound, while Mr White was composing a Dictionary or some other book for the study of Latin. If a boy through nervousness twitched his face or moved his tongue into his cheek, and was caught by the master's eye, Mr White roared at him, accused him of making grimaces at his master, and ordered him to keep on doing the same nervous action for half an hour. On one occasion I was roared at. After the dismissal of the class I returned to the study and said, "I did not mean to offend you." He said "All right," continued his notes, and I retired. Not long afterwards he roared again, and I mentioned the affair to my parents, and it got, through a friend, to the ears of Mr Whitbread, a Governor of Christ's Hospital. This was not what I had intended, but I was not sorry. The reason that schoolboys do not make complaints of ill treatment is not, as is sometimes supposed, a noble hatred of talebearing superior to that which is found in grown-up persons, but it is that they know that complaints will probably do them more harm than good, for it is impossible for boys to obtain a fair hearing. Mr Whitbread called for me on Speech Day, and said, "You are a little donkey." I replied, in my thoughts but not aloud, "And you are a big one, probably not trained to be civil as I have been, so I make allowance for you." I thought again that notwithstanding this rudeness, he might have done me a good turn, and, in that case, I would feel grateful to him. Well, so it turned out, for the next time I went to the Latin School, Mr White said before the class that henceforth he and I were going to be friends; and with a seeming contradiction, that he should not speak to me again. In future, when he heard the class, he should pass me over. He said this with a smiling face, and added that he supposed there was fraternity between the brewer, Mr Whitbread, and me, because my name, Butler, is associated with wine.

Occasionally Mr White was most affable to the boys. Once full of apparent friendliness, he asked a multitude of questions about the things in Mr Fletcher's

---

[5] Alexander Cruden (1699-1770).

Tuck-shop, which was in the "Garden". Unlike St Paul, who when he became a man "put away childish things", Mr White became more childish than the boys before him. He expressed a desire to learn from them the exact shape of the cornered tarts, the size and flavour of the High pies, the Low pies, the jumbles, packets of cocoa, sherbet and the rest. When all his questions were fully satisfied, he exclaimed to the class, who were half ashamed and half amused, but obliged to answer, "Well, boys, you certainly show great knowledge of these things. I am surprised at your information; if you took the same interest in your Latin, we should do well!" Sometime he broke the silence of the study by exclaiming over this composition, "There dear little notes! If a boy does not learn from them he ought to be flogged."

Once, when nearing the end of the afternoon school hours, he put down his pen, rubbed his hands together, and fell back in the chair laughing. With a face beaming with smiles he told us that he had finished his day's work, and now was going home to his dinner. And, as if to make all <u>lash</u>, that is, long for what we could not have, he described to us what the items of the dinner would be. "Roast beef and rich gravy. Delicious! Potatoes, either roasted crisp under the meat or if boiled, well done and floury. Very nice! Yorkshire pudding rich and brown. Ah! After that, fruit-pie with light flaky crust and plenty of delightful juice! custard and a glass of wine!" Here he gave us a merry roguish look, which seemed to say, What do you think of that, boys? Wouldn't you like the tuck-in that I'm going to have? When you are at your miserable housy meal, I shall be enjoying myself.

Chapter 19. WARD X

When the great Pigging took place, I was pigged from Ward XV to Ward X, of which the Nurse, now called Matron, was Mrs Downing. All the Nurses were turned into Matrons at this time. A thing that is worthy to be recorded happened after the pigging. Whether or not it arose from ill-feeling between the Grammar School Wards and the Latin School Wards, I cannot say, but so it was that they behaved like foolish dogs, which Dr Watts tells children not to imitate. They fight for no discoverable reason. First for some time the opposed Wards saved up all the orange peel they could get, and had a battle with that. I did not join in the folly for I never liked anything ill-bred or rough. However I did not grudge the encounter to those who could enjoy it, for although ill-mannered it was almost harmless. I thought that if the English, Russians and French fought with orange peel, no great harm would be done. This idea led to another. If gentlemen and ladies who love to be cruel to foxes and even breed them to hunt them to death with hounds would have a meet for the purpose of stamping on cockroaches, their time would be better employed. But I was wrong. Such insipid and questionable cruelty would not thoroughly satisfy them. They would wish to destroy things more charming and graceful than cockroaches, to say nothing of the pleasure of glutting their brutal appetite with the sight of blood and pain.[6]

The orange-peel battle was not satisfactory, because it was not mischievous. The only result was that the combatants returned to their Wards with yellow faces. What was to be done? They must have a real cruel battle although there was no cause for it, and no sense in it. For some time in No. X I saw lads making most dangerous weapons. I recollect that there were sticks with leaden buttons and bullets attached to the end of them. Happily, the fight never took place. I was informed that the authorities of Christ's Hospital heard about the affair, and caused several of the big lads to take their oath that they would not fight, and so the matter ended.

One of the lads of this Ward, D., had a vile temper. He opened a pocketknife,

---

[6] TRB was a vegetarian, following in this as in Esperanto the example of his son Christie, who became a vegetarian in 1895 at the age of 12, after visiting a slaughter-house.

and stabbed in the back a boy who had offended him. The wounded one fell down insensible and was placed on a bed by those near and was thought by them to be dead. A lad went to the Matron at the other end of the Ward, and told her, "Please, Mum, D. has killed a boy." "D.", cried she. "Yes, Mum." "Come here. Do you know, D., what you have done? Do you know, D., that you have killed a boy?" "I don't care, he shouldn't have aggravated me." "D. you'll be 'anged. I shouldn't like to be you, D., you'll be 'anged." Fortunately, after a while, the boys were able to tell her, "Please, Mum, N. is not dead." Then she said, "And a very good thing it is for you, D., that N. is not dead, for you would 'ave been 'anged. As sure as you stand 'ere, you would 'ave been 'anged."

After I had been some time in this Ward, a notice was given that a confirmation would be held in the Church on a certain week day. Those who were to be confirmed were of course excused from School for the necessary Church service, and as no questions were asked and there was no personal interview required, it was deemed better to go to church than to school, apart from any religious consideration with regard to the affair. As to preparation, there was one gathering in the Hall before Dr Jacob, and one gathering before Mrs Downing, the Matron, the latter of course for our Ward, No.X. Dr Jacob's words were so feeble that I wondered how he became a Doctor of Divinity. What the Matron said was much better. Indeed I felt that it would be hard, though I was fond of reading religious treatises, to expect any theological knowledge from her. I thought a question she asked was good – "If you were to die now, where would you go?" It is a question too seldom asked by clergymen in their sermons. She did her best to perform a solemn duty. We were on forms arranged as at a Sunday School and she sat in front of us. This is what I remember:-

"My dear boys, You are going to be confirmed, and you are quite right to be confirmed now you have the opportunity. We never know when we shall die; we might die this very instant, and we ought to be prepared for death. But, S., are you going to be confirmed? M. Is a good boy and is fit to be confirmed, but you are not, I am sure. Why! You give me a great deal of trouble. Only a short time ago you forgot to bring your flannel from the lavatory. Well! I am surprised! Confirmation is a very solemn thing and I want you all to think what a dreadful thing it is to die unprepared. Young persons die as well as the older, and sometimes quite suddenly. Where would you go? It's too dreadful to think of."

Sometimes the monotony of School life was interrupted by attempts to run away from Christ's Hospital. Three lads of this Ward, M., L., and D. agreed to do so. Some time before the day they fixed, they made rope ladders to climb forest trees, and they purposed to buy a half-crown pistol to shoot rabbits and also to provide themselves with a tin pot in which to make blackberry-jam over a fire of forest wood. But it was essential that they should have towny clothes and these they were busy making every day, D. excepted, who gave no help at all. The trousers and coats were cut out of white calico, and the sewing was such as is seen in tacking. I thought that forest life would immediately tear them to pieces. I could not imagine how L., whom I had always known as a cripple, could climb rope ladders. It was true he was stronger than he had been at Hertford, where he required the help of surgical apparatus and crutches, but he was still somewhat lame.

The Matron and Monitors did not see the preparations: when they approached, everything was instantly hidden. Well, the time arrived for M., L., and D.'s departure. Antony, the Beadle who guarded one of the entrances of the School, was informed by a lad they sent to him that the Treasurer was walking round the corner of a cloister close by, and wished to speak to him at once. Antony turned his back to the gate-portal, and the runaways made their escape. In the evening, D. came back to the School with his pockets and arms full of good things. He had brought them from his home, which was a confectioner's shop. D. had deceived his companions. From the first he did not intend to go with them. He had schemed an opportunity of getting a day's outing. This was evident because directly he got outside the Hospital he left them and went home. In those days the quick discovery of the whereabouts of a person missing was not provided by electrical invention; however, after M. and L. had stayed away for two or three days, they were found and brought back by the police. The two runaways were "brushed" (birched) but not in public. The doctor allowed the authorities to give the lad with weak limbs six strokes not too hard. D., I think, was not punished at all. He was probably regarded by the authorities as a penitent who set a good example to his companions which they refused to follow.

I asked L. to give me an account of his excursion. He treated me to a long yarn, over which we both laughed, but which I secretly regarded as mostly fiction. The first night, he said, was spent under a cart turned upside down. He and his companion slept all right, and afterwards they trespassed on a farmer's field and were chased. They narrowly escaped a pitchfork which was thrown after them. They made some blackberry jam in their tin pot. This I did not believe, but I did not tell him so. I enquired whether or not he thought the pleasures of the excursion made amends for the brushing. "As to the brushing," L. replied, "the good breakfast I had at the police station, the new towny bread, hot coffee, good butter, and as much of all as we wished, more than made up for the brushing. I would gladly, if I could, go away again for such another breakfast."

I shall now give the Reader a specimen of the magging lectures of Mrs Downing on the subject of leaving the flannel in the Lavatory. It had so many repetitions that it sounded like a tedious tune with too many <u>Dal Seono's</u> in it. "You're not a very good boy to leave your flannel in the Lavatory. No, you give me a great deal of trouble. Is that good – to give trouble? I say it isn't, it's <u>naughty</u>. I., you are a naughty boy. I am ashamed of you: you ought to be ashamed of yourself. I call such conduct <u>wicked</u>. You naughty boy! You naughty wicked sinful boy! Shame! And you want to make me think that you are good. That's <u>'ypocritical</u>. One who is sinful and pretends to be good is a 'ypocrite. You naughty wicked sinful 'ypocrite! Shame! I say again, Shame! And your father's a clergyman, too! Poor man! I pity him. After all 'is trouble and care to train you up to be a good son, you become instead a naught wicked sinful 'ypocrite. What a disappointment! Poor man! I pity him! Shame! What swords and daggers it must be in 'is 'eart to 'ave such a wicked son!"

She had a sense of humour, for when she found that one of the boys had not been listening, but had been fast asleep through all her mag, she smiled. It had lasted a whole hour. And if the Reader wishes to make it last that time, he can, like her, do so by repetitions of her phrases and exclamations <u>ad nauseam</u> with long pauses and movements of the hand. After all this waste of time, the hour for sitting up is fully spent, and the Matron says, "You must go to bed now." "Please, Mum, I shall get caned if I don't do my imposition." "Go to bed, go to bed, go to bed."

One of the amusements of the Ward was an Apple Pie Bed. An Apple Pie Bed was a bed made over again on its owner's absence, the sheet on which one lies being turned back to the head of the bed, so that when the owner of the bed tried to get into it, he found that he could not. We then had a laugh, and asked him what he was doing.

Another joke was with a bolio (bolster). A lad arranged in the twilight, by a string he placed unobserved along the ground, to pull away the bolio of another lad in the middle of the night. Say there were two beds, 9 and 45, each in an opposite row. The beds were at a long distance from each other, but had no impediment between them. In the night the occupant of 45 held one end of the string and the other end was tied to one end of the bolio of 9. When the occupant of Bed 9 was fast asleep, the boy lying in 45 jerked the string occasionally until the occupant of 9 was disturbed, and finally became half awakened. The half-awakened lad lifted his head, looked at his bolio, and finding it was still as usual, concluded that he had been dreaming, and laid his head down on it again. The boy in 45 again jerked the string, and while the bolio was being examined by the now three-quarters awakened boy, drew it slowly out of the bed 9 on to the floor. As it moved down the pathway between the two rows of beds its owner crawled after it, patting it as it moved, just as a cat would pat a mouse. The bolio seemed to be alive. This thing was evidently a great mystery. It was very remarkable that it should run without legs, and not like any other live thing, not even move in the manner of a worm. Why it should suddenly in the middle of the night take a fancy to leave its station, and make an excursion down the Ward was strange indeed.

CHRIST'S HOSPITAL, LONDON

Chapter 20. THE CHURCH

A weekly change from the inside walls was the Sunday Divine Service at the Church, and the Foundation provided every boy with a Bible and Prayer Book bound together. The Church adjoined the School. There was something dubious about this gratification. Everything in the service was conducted in a tedious manner. We knelt on hard wooden benches without any support before or behind, which was painful to the kiddies, especially during the Litany. I never fainted, but the fear that I should faint made me nervous and sometimes lads did faint owing to the severity. There was a Deputy Grecian Monitor, D., sitting in the Church in front of Ward XV, who used to say, "Kneel up" to any lad who showed a sign of fatigue. He told us that he was a High Churchman, and that those who showed signs of fatigue were like Dissenters. "Dissenters" he explained, "are fat persons who do not kneel at prayer." But this foolish youth forgot to observe that he himself did not kneel at all, but sat comfortably in Church in a seat with a back to it. The name of the Incumbent of the Church was the Rev. Michael Gibbs. He was a great authority on the subject of Queen Anne's Bounty.[7] When I had ceased to be a Blue Coat boy, and had become a clergyman I heard him give a lecture at a Ruri-decanal meeting on this subject. Several of his hearers were clergymen of great learning, but after he had spoken, no one ventured to say a word or ask a question. His pulpit utterances at Christ Church when I was at C. H. were couched in polite and courtly language and patiently read through in a uniform tone and manner. There is only one thing of interest that he said which is fixed on my mind. A sudden pause occurred in one of his sermons. He uttered these solemn words, "Awake thou sleeper." Another pause. Then he continued. It was as if a kettle, suddenly removed from the fire, ceased to hum, and being put back again to the fire, again continued its lulling song. I am reminded of one of Hogarth's pictures in which a maiden is represented as having during the sermon attempted to read the marriage service. There it is in an open book on her lap, and she is fast asleep.

We went to Church also on other days in the week on important Holy Days, and for services of national importance. Among the latter was the 5th of November

---

[7] A fund established in 1704 "for the Augmentation of the Maintenance of Poor Clergy".

thanksgiving for the escape from the Gunpowder Treason and the arrival of King William and the 30th January, a Fast of the execution of "the Blessed King Charles the First", in the service for which there is a fabricated Psalm of various scripture texts. This Psalm, though extremely laughable, excites admiration for its ingenuity. It reminds me of an insect cleverly concocted out of the parts of several insects by some entomologists who wished to play a prank on a learned professor. They asked him to name it. He looked at it for a few seconds through a microscope, and said, without smiling, "The name of it is Humbug." Then, too, there was the Confirmation Service. There must have been a Bishop at my confirmation, and I must have come down from where I was sitting by the side of the Organ in the Gallery in order to be blessed by him, but I have no recollection of him and the service, except that it was an extremely dull affair and almost out of my sight and hearing. But I spent the time profitably. S. Who sat next to me, was an Atheist, and I did my utmost to convince him that there is a God.

CHRIST'S HOSPITAL, LONDON

Chapter 21. A LEAVE DAY

Once a month at Christ's Hospital there was a Leave Day, that is, a day on which the scholars might go outside the walls of the Foundation for the whole day to see their relations and friends, or do what they liked. There was a time in the evening fixed for their return. A quarter of an hour's grace was allowed, but if a boy came back five minutes after this grace, he was entered by the Beadles at the Gate as twenty minutes late, and much time was deducted from his next Leaveday.

The Reader may ask, Did the Ancient, Worshipful and Royal Foundation provide any treat for its scholars. Yes, on one of the days after Easter we were all marched to the Mansion House with a paper pinned on our coat with the words "He is risen" and received from the Lord Mayor the gift of a new shilling, two buns and a glass of either port or sherry wine.

There was a provision for a bath once or twice in the summer outside Christ's Hospital at the Peerless Pool.[8] The water there was very cold, and we dreaded it when we passed through the entrance called "Funk Alley".

Christ's Hospital boys liked to pay diligent attention to their appearance. They kept the coat well brushed, the bands clean and firm as the starch had made them, pressed them between the leaves of a book, cleaned and polished the girdle, and rubbed the silver buckle with whiting. In London a broad girdle, indented with stars, and clasped by a silver buckle was seen not only on the Grecians and monitors but on most of the elder scholars. Before play they buttoned the coat over the bands and wore an old thin girdle (putting the respectable girdle away) and tucked into the old thin girdle the coat-skirt. This, in Bible language, would be girding up one's loins. After play, the white bands and bright red girdle and silver buckle reappeared. Then with well-brushed

---

[8] The Peerless Pool was London's first outdoor swimming pool. Originally it was called the "Perilous Pond", on account of so many people drowning there. According to some authorities it closed in 1850 and was built over, but that cannot be correct, since TRB only began to attend the London school in 1853. Also dubious, given the reference to Funk Alley, are the observations of William Hone in 1826: "Every fine Thursday and Saturday afternoon in the summer columns of Bluecoat boys, more than a score in each, headed by their respective beadles, arrive and some half strip themselves 'ere they reach their destination. The rapid plunges they make into the Pool and their hilarity in the bath testify their enjoyment of the tepid fluid."

boots, coloured kid gloves and a beautiful white handkerchief showing from the pocket they looked on a holiday little swells. In the old-fashioned Victorian days, it was very important that a gentleman should not go out of a house into the gaze of the public without kid gloves, and as it was wrong to shake hands with a gloved hand, and one might meet a friend, it was well to carry the right-hand glove in the left hand so as not to keep him waiting for a handshake. The neat appearance of the Blue-Coat boy, and the glow of his face did not show, as some outsiders imagine, that he had plenty of food, was not hungry, and enjoyed good health. The boys soon spent the few pence they received from home, and if anyone gave them a tip, they never felt it to be <u>infra dig</u> to receive it. On the contrary, they were grateful to the donor, generally an Old Blue, and loved him for his kindness. When I was on my way to my home in South Kensington, I asked a gentleman the time of day. He gave me a shilling, and told me that he had been a Bluecoat boy. On another Leave Day at the Zoological Gardens with two other Blues, one of them an elder brother, an Old Blue gave us sixpence each. We were, however, unfortunate. We, all three, bought the same kind of meat pie which was unpalatable. We got rid of our pies by feeding a wild pig, saying to it, "Eat your poor brother."

On another Leave Day my brother and I went to the Crystal Palace. The Nurse of our Ward XV happened to go there too. We heard her say to a Bluecoat boy of the Ward. "Why! Is it you, M.? How you've grown! I hardly knew you. You <u>have</u> grown!" This puzzled us. It seemed strange that a boy should grow very much in so short a time, for the nurse had seen all of us that same day in the morning. We talked the matter over and came to the conclusion that she must have suddenly thought just for the moment that it was the holidays not a Leave Day.

Another place of amusement was the Tower. The boys of C.H. could enter <u>gratis</u>. The charge to the public for entrance was a shilling. We took little interest in it, and I put off my visit to the last day possible for me to enjoy my privilege. I thought it a "mouldy" place.

I often spent part of my Leave Day in the Lambeth Baths. The water was pleasantly tepid, and in the midst of the swimming bath there was a fountain of delicious warm water. There we could take a rest when tired and prepare for another swim. Sanders, after a dive, could move like a fish close to the bottom a considerable part of the length of the Bath.

This place so delighted me that nine nights running I dreamt I was swimming.

TOM BUTLER'S SCHOOLDAYS

Chapter 21. CONCLUSION

Time passed slowly, or seemed to do so. The year 1857, in which, according to Dr. Cumming's prophecy, the world was in all probability to come to an end, came and passed.[9] Nothing special happened. I was thinking about the prophecy when I was in the Cloister before the Hall door, having the Bluecoat School Cap on my head. Mr Brooks inspected us the certify that the cap was used. Two events happened in the years about this time. One was an eclipse of the sun which was invisible to us and disappointing, for a holiday was given to us and we all wasted our time waiting to see it, and spent a penny at Mr Fletcher's shop on a piece of red glass through which to behold it. The other event was the passage through the sky of a large comet with an immense tail, I think in the year 1861.[10] In this year I became on the 10th of June 15 years of age, which was the date for me to leave Christ's Hospital.

I left the Ancient and Royal Foundation four days before my time for no reason excepting that my Father at my request asked permission, and my desire was granted.

After leaving the School I went to other Schools, had private tutors, and, inspired by a book, "The Student's Guide", studied fervently many subjects.[11] By this time, very fortunately for me, the oculist-profession had invented spectacles to suit my sight, and for a short time I went to a Bank. I kept up acquaintance with my Old Blue friends for a time. I saw Green at Boston where he was a Bank Clerk. Jeffery visited me in South Kensington at my Father's house. Sanders called upon me at my College, Highbury, where for three years I was trained in Holy Orders. I met him again at Bethnal Green. Afterwards my duties as a clergyman took me to various parts of the country, and in the long time that followed I gradually lost my knowledge of these Bluecoat boys altogether.

It is suggested by a friend that I should make a comparison between Christ's Hospital in my time and Christ's Hospital in the present days, but this I cannot do, as I cannot undertake to re-enter the world and school again in order to have experience of the present. Everything everywhere, I am told, has improved, and

---

[9] Dr. John Cumming (1807-81).

[10] Presumably the Great Comet Tebbut.

[11] *The Student's Guide, designed by Specific directions to aid in forming and strengthening the intellectual and moral character and habits of the student*, by the Rev. *John Todd with all the Latin quotations translated*(1839). Later, abridged versions were published under the title *Self-Improvement*.

CHRIST'S HOSPITAL, LONDON

therefore at Christ's Hospital. I am quite ready to believe this, if told so by another for it is what I earnestly wish, but general hearsay I cannot state as a matter of my own knowledge. I asked for an instance of improvement, and was told that now Christ's Hospital boys are allowed to wear towny clothes in the Holidays. But I cannot decide that this is an improvement. Does the Christ's Hospital boy of the present generation dislike his dress? It is comfortable. We, Christ's Hospital scholars of the old time, had no objection to the humour of the City Arabs who called after us; it simply amused us. Do the girls of today want to dress like boys? If they do, would the change be an improvement? I must leave these questions for the present generation to decide. A more important question is:- is brutality and selfishness in the world giving place to gentleness and lovingkindness? In spite of exceptions I am glad to think that on the whole there is a gradual improvement which will continue to take place in the great mass of our British nation and those nations which have sprung from her, and that eventually it will be a model for imitation by the rest of the world.

END OF CHRIST'S HOSPITAL, LONDON.

PUBLIC SUPPER OF THE SCHOLARS AT CHRIST'S HOSPITAL.

TOM BUTLER'S SCHOOLDAYS

www.ingramcontent.com/pod-product-compliance
Lightning Source LLC
Chambersburg PA
CBHW061459040426
42450CB00008B/1424